EMDR HANDBOOK

Transform Your Life with Self-Help Techniques to Relieve Stress, Overcome Anxiety, Build Meaningful Relationships, and Achieve Emotional Freedom Every Day

D1707987

Emerson Monroe

Table of Contents

Introduction

Chapter 1: Understanding EMDR

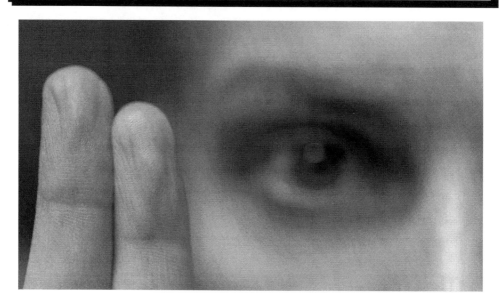

1.1: A Brief History of EMDR Therapy

Eye Movement Desensitization and Reprocessing (EMDR) therapy originated in the late 1980s when psychologist Francine Shapiro made a serendipitous discovery while walking in a park. Shapiro noticed that eye movements appeared to decrease the negative emotion associated with her own distressing memories. Intrigued by this observation, she began to systematically study the effects of eye movements on the emotional intensity of traumatic memories. Her initial research, published in 1989, provided the first empirical evidence for the efficacy of what she termed EMDR therapy in the treatment of Post-Traumatic Stress Disorder (PTSD).

The foundational principle of EMDR therapy is based on the Adaptive Information Processing (AIP) model, which posits that distressing memories are inadequately processed by the brain, leading to maladaptive responses. EMDR therapy aims to facilitate the accessing and processing of traumatic memories to bring about adaptive resolution. Through a structured eight-phase approach, therapists guide clients in recalling distressing images while simultaneously focusing on an external stimulus, typically bilateral eye movements, taps, or tones.

From its inception, EMDR therapy has undergone rigorous scientific scrutiny. Over the years, a substantial body of research has emerged, validating its effectiveness not only for PTSD but also for a range of psychological stressors and conditions, including anxiety, depression, and phobias. This expansion of applicability reflects the therapy's underlying premise that the way the brain processes information can be altered to achieve therapeutic goals.

The evolution of EMDR therapy from a novel observation to a scientifically supported treatment modality is a testament to the dynamic nature of psychological research and practice. Shapiro's development of EMDR therapy has been characterized by an openness to new insights and empirical validation, leading to its recognition as an effective treatment by major psychological and psychiatric associations worldwide.

EMDR therapy's journey from an incidental finding to a cornerstone of trauma therapy underscores the importance of innovation and evidence-based practice in the field of psychology. As it continues to evolve, EMDR therapy remains a powerful tool for healing, offering hope and relief to those burdened by the weight of traumatic memories.

1.2: Target Audience and Benefits

This handbook is designed to serve as a comprehensive guide for three primary groups: patients experiencing psychological distress, therapists seeking to expand their therapeutic toolkit, and individuals committed to personal growth and well-being. Each group stands to gain unique benefits from the insights and techniques shared within these pages, tailored to their specific needs and objectives.

Patients grappling with stress, anxiety, or the aftermath of traumatic events will find solace in the detailed explanation of how Eye Movement Desensitization and Reprocessing (EMDR) therapy can facilitate emotional healing. This book demystifies the scientific principles behind EMDR, making it accessible to those without a background in psychology. By presenting step-by-step self-help techniques inspired by EMDR principles, it empowers individuals to actively participate in their recovery process, offering them strategies to manage and alleviate symptoms outside the therapy room.

Therapists and mental health professionals will discover a valuable resource in the exploration of EMDR's applications beyond the treatment of PTSD. The book outlines how this therapy can be integrated into a broader therapeutic approach, enhancing their practice by providing new avenues for addressing a wide range of psychological issues. It emphasizes the importance of a nuanced understanding of the Adaptive Information Processing (AIP) model and offers insights into tailoring EMDR techniques to the needs of diverse clients, thereby improving therapeutic outcomes.

Seekers of well-being, those curious about self-improvement and personal development, will find the handbook a treasure trove of techniques for cultivating emotional resilience, improving interpersonal relationships, and achieving a more balanced life. It introduces EMDR-inspired exercises that can be practiced independently to reduce daily stress, overcome emotional blocks, and foster a deeper sense of connection with oneself and others. The book encourages a proactive approach to mental health, emphasizing the role of self-care and mindfulness in achieving emotional freedom.

For all readers, this handbook emphasizes the transformative potential of EMDR, not only as a therapeutic tool for overcoming trauma but also as a powerful method for personal growth and emotional well-being. It offers a clear, accessible introduction to the theory behind EMDR, practical guidance for applying its principles, and encouragement to explore its benefits in various aspects of life. Through detailed explanations, practical exercises, and real-life examples, the book aims to equip individuals with the knowledge and tools needed to embark on a journey toward healing, growth, and emotional liberation.

1.3: Using This Handbook Effectively

To harness the full potential of this handbook, approach it with an open mind and a commitment to apply its principles in your daily life. Begin by familiarizing yourself with the foundational concepts of EMDR therapy presented in the initial chapters. These sections lay the groundwork, explaining the science behind the method and its distinctive benefits compared to traditional therapeutic approaches.

Moving forward, each chapter is structured to progressively build your understanding and skills. The book is divided into parts that address different aspects of EMDR, from scientific explanations to practical self-help techniques. For those seeking to alleviate stress, manage anxiety, or enhance personal relationships, focus on the chapters dedicated to these topics. They provide step-by-step guides, practical exercises, and real-life applications of EMDR principles.

For a more hands-on experience, the latter part of the book introduces self-practice techniques inspired by EMDR therapy. These sections are crucial for readers aiming to apply the therapy's methods to their own lives. Detailed instructions for bilateral tapping, guided visualizations, and strategies for overcoming emotional blocks are presented in an easy-to-follow format. Practice these exercises regularly, noting any changes in your emotional state or stress levels.

Additionally, the book includes chapters on integrating EMDR into daily routines and using it to build emotional resilience. These sections offer strategies for making EMDR a part of your holistic approach to wellness, alongside mindfulness, meditation, and other complementary therapies.

To maximize the benefits, engage actively with the exercises, reflect on your experiences in a journal, and be patient with your progress. EMDR is a powerful tool, but like any therapeutic technique, it requires time and practice to see transformational results.

Remember, this handbook is designed to be a resource you can return to time and again. As your understanding deepens or your needs change, different sections will offer new insights and strategies. Keep this book accessible, and allow it to guide you through your journey toward emotional freedom and well-being.

Chapter 2: Why EMDR is Different

2.1: EMDR vs. Traditional Therapy

EMDR (Eye Movement Desensitization and Reprocessing) significantly diverges from traditional therapy modalities in its approach to treating psychological distress. Unlike conventional therapies that primarily focus on talk therapy and cognitive interventions, EMDR introduces an innovative method that directly impacts the way memories are processed by the brain. This distinction is crucial for understanding why EMDR can be particularly effective for individuals who have found limited relief in other forms of therapy.

Firstly, the core of EMDR therapy revolves around its unique use of bilateral stimulation, typically through guided eye movements, to facilitate the brain's natural healing processes. This method is based on the premise that psychological stress is often the result of unprocessed traumatic memories. By activating both hemispheres of the brain, EMDR aims to unlock and reprocess these memories, reducing their emotional impact and allowing for cognitive restructuring to occur. This contrasts sharply with traditional talk therapies that may not directly engage the brain's innate mechanisms for processing distressing memories.

Secondly, EMDR therapy is structured around an eight-phase protocol that includes phases of stabilization, memory processing, and integration. This structured approach ensures that clients are not only prepared for the reprocessing of traumatic memories but also supported in integrating positive cognitive shifts into their daily lives. Traditional therapies may not offer this level of structured support for dealing with traumatic memories, often focusing more on coping mechanisms and less on resolving the root causes of distress.

Furthermore, EMDR therapy emphasizes the non-verbal processing of memories, which can be particularly beneficial for individuals who struggle to articulate their experiences or for whom talking about their trauma is retraumatizing. This aspect of EMDR allows for healing to occur at a deeper, neurological level, beyond the limitations of verbal expression. In contrast, traditional therapies often rely heavily on verbal communication as the primary tool for healing, which may not be suitable for all clients.

Another key difference is the speed at which EMDR can bring about relief and change. Many clients report significant improvements in their symptoms after just a few sessions of EMDR therapy. This rapid effectiveness is attributed to the direct way EMDR targets the brain's information processing system, offering a quicker path to resolving emotional distress than the typically longer courses of treatment associated with traditional therapies.

Lastly, EMDR's versatility stands out. Originally developed for PTSD, its application has expanded to include a wide range of psychological issues, including anxiety, depression, and phobias. This adaptability showcases EMDR's fundamental difference from traditional therapies, which may have more limited scopes or require different approaches for various conditions.

In summary, EMDR distinguishes itself from traditional therapy through its unique focus on bilateral stimulation, structured protocol, non-verbal processing, rapid effectiveness, and versatility in treating various psychological conditions. These key differences underscore why EMDR has become a valuable tool in the field of mental health, offering new hope and pathways to healing for many individuals.

2.2: EMDR for Everyday Stress and Personal Growth

EMDR, or Eye Movement Desensitization and Reprocessing, extends its benefits far beyond the realms of treating severe trauma. Its efficacy in addressing everyday stress, mild anxiety, and personal growth is grounded in its unique approach to processing memories and emotions. The technique is not limited to those with profound traumatic experiences; rather, it offers a versatile tool for anyone seeking to enhance their emotional well-being and navigate the complexities of daily life.

At the heart of EMDR's universal applicability is the Adaptive Information Processing (AIP) model, which suggests that much of our emotional distress stems from unprocessed memories, not necessarily of traumatic events but also of everyday stressors and anxieties. These memories, when inadequately processed by our brain, can influence our current emotional responses and behaviors in ways that may seem disproportionate or unexplainable. EMDR facilitates the reprocessing of these memories, allowing for a reduction in emotional distress and an improvement in psychological health.

For individuals experiencing daily stress, EMDR offers a pathway to process these stressors more adaptively. Stressful memories, such as workplace conflicts or financial worries, can be targeted and reprocessed, leading to a decrease in overall stress levels. This reprocessing aids in viewing past and present stressors with new perspectives, fostering a sense of calm and resilience in the face of life's challenges.

In terms of anxiety, whether it's generalized anxiety disorder, social anxiety, or mild situational anxiety, EMDR can help. By focusing on specific memories that contribute to one's anxiety, EMDR works to desensitize the individual to these triggers, reducing the intensity of anxious responses. This process not only alleviates symptoms of anxiety but also contributes to a more grounded and confident approach to situations that previously provoked anxiety.

Personal growth is another significant area where EMDR proves beneficial. By reprocessing past experiences that may subconsciously influence one's self-esteem, decision-making, and worldview, individuals can unlock new levels of self-awareness and confidence. This newfound perspective can lead to improved interpersonal relationships, better decision-making skills, and a deeper sense of personal fulfillment.

Moreover, the versatility of EMDR means it can be adapted to suit a wide range of personal objectives and emotional challenges. Whether it's enhancing performance in professional settings, improving communication in relationships, or cultivating a more positive outlook on life, EMDR provides a framework for emotional and psychological growth.

It's important to note that while EMDR can be a powerful tool for self-help and personal development, the guidance of a trained EMDR therapist is invaluable, especially when dealing with more complex or deeply rooted issues. However, for everyday stress and mild anxiety, self-administered techniques inspired by EMDR principles can also offer significant benefits.

In conclusion, EMDR's applicability to a broad spectrum of emotional and psychological issues makes it a valuable resource not only for those recovering from trauma but also for anyone seeking to improve their mental health, navigate daily stresses more effectively, and pursue personal growth. Its foundation in the AIP model provides a scientific basis for its effectiveness across a range of scenarios, making it a versatile and powerful tool in the quest for emotional freedom and well-being.

Chapter 3: The Promise of This Book

3.1: Overcoming Anxiety and Relational Challenges

Creating a **safe space** is fundamental in the practice of EMDR, serving as a cornerstone for individuals looking to alleviate anxiety, manage stress, and enhance their interpersonal relationships. This concept, rooted in psychological safety, allows individuals to explore and process emotions without fear of judgment or harm. It's especially pertinent for those embarking on a journey toward emotional freedom, providing a secure mental environment where healing and personal growth can flourish.

Grounding techniques are practical tools designed to anchor individuals in the present moment, mitigating the physiological and emotional symptoms of stress and anxiety. These techniques, ranging from deep breathing exercises to sensory engagement practices, play a pivotal role in establishing a safe space. They are easily accessible and can be seamlessly integrated into daily routines, offering immediate relief in moments of distress.

1. **Visualization of a Safe Place**:
   This exercise encourages individuals to conjure a mental image of a place that evokes feelings of security and calmness. By focusing on the sensory details of this imagined environment, such as the sounds, sights, and smells, individuals can create a mental refuge accessible during times of anxiety or stress.

2. **Breathing Techniques for Relaxation**:
   Deep, controlled breathing acts as a powerful tool in regulating the body's stress response. Techniques such as the 4-7-8 method or diaphragmatic breathing can help lower heart rate and promote a sense of calm, making them invaluable components of a safe space.

3. **Positive Affirmations for Safety**:
   The use of affirmations can reinforce a sense of security and self-compassion. Repeating phrases like "I am safe" or "I am in control" can help challenge and alleviate negative thoughts, contributing to a protective mental environment.

4. **Grounding Techniques for Stability**:
   Engaging the five senses through grounding techniques can provide immediate distraction from overwhelming emotions, bringing the individual back to the present. Simple actions like holding a cold ice cube, savoring a piece of candy, or touching a textured surface can be remarkably effective in reducing anxiety.

5. **Creating a Personal Sanctuary**:
   This exercise involves designing a personalized safe space, incorporating elements that provide comfort and reassurance. Whether it's a cozy corner of a room or a detailed mental construct, this sanctuary serves as a bastion of tranquility amidst the chaos of daily life.

Incorporating these exercises into one's self-care regimen can significantly enhance the ability to cope with anxiety, stress, and relational challenges. By establishing a safe space, individuals not only safeguard their emotional well-being but also lay the groundwork for meaningful personal development and healthier relationships. Through the application of grounding techniques and the cultivation of a protective mental environment, the promise of achieving emotional freedom becomes an attainable reality for anyone committed to their journey of self-improvement.

3.2: The Journey Toward Emotional Freedom

Achieving emotional freedom is a transformative process that involves both understanding the theoretical underpinnings of Eye Movement Desensitization and Reprocessing (EMDR) and applying its practical techniques. This section delves into how individuals can embark on this path, leveraging EMDR to navigate through the complexities of stress, anxiety, and interpersonal difficulties, ultimately leading to a state of emotional liberation.

At the core of EMDR therapy is the Adaptive Information Processing (AIP) model, which posits that psychological stress and anxiety are often the result of unprocessed traumatic memories. These memories can cause disruptions in emotional functioning. Understanding this model is crucial as it provides a framework for why and how EMDR facilitates the processing of these memories, allowing for emotional healing.

The first step in this journey involves identifying specific memories or current situations that trigger emotional distress. This self-awareness is pivotal as it directs the focus of the EMDR therapy. Individuals can begin by journaling their experiences, emotions, and reactions to uncover patterns and triggers. This introspective practice is not only therapeutic but also instrumental in tailoring the EMDR process to address personal emotional hurdles.

Subsequently, the application of bilateral stimulation, a hallmark of EMDR therapy, comes into play. This technique can be adapted for self-help through simplified practices such as bilateral tapping. By alternately tapping the left and right sides of the body, individuals can mimic the eye movement patterns used in professional EMDR therapy sessions. This action helps to stimulate the brain's information processing system, facilitating the reprocessing of stuck memories.

Incorporating visualization techniques further enhances the journey toward emotional freedom. Individuals are encouraged to visualize a safe place where they feel secure and at peace. This mental imagery, combined with bilateral stimulation, creates a dual focus that aids in the processing of traumatic memories without overwhelming the individual. It's a practice that not only addresses past traumas but also equips individuals with a tool for managing future stressors.

Positive affirmations play a supportive role in this process. Replacing negative beliefs and self-talk with positive affirmations can reinforce the changes in emotional responses triggered by EMDR. Phrases such as "I am worthy of healing" or "I am becoming more resilient every day" can be powerful motivators and reminders of the progress being made.

Lastly, it's essential to recognize that emotional freedom does not imply the absence of negative emotions. Rather, it signifies a state where individuals possess the tools and resilience to navigate through life's challenges without being unduly hindered by past traumas or current anxieties. Regular practice of EMDR-inspired techniques, mindfulness, and self-compassion are key to maintaining and advancing this state of emotional well-being.

By combining a theoretical understanding of EMDR with these practical self-help techniques, individuals can embark on a fulfilling path toward emotional freedom. This process is not linear but a continual journey of self-discovery, healing, and growth. With dedication and practice, the promise of emotional liberation becomes an achievable reality, fostering a life of greater peace, fulfillment, and emotional resilience.

Part 1: Understanding EMDR

Chapter 4: The Science Behind EMDR

4.1: Understanding the AIP Model in EMDR

The **Adaptive Information Processing (AIP)** model is the theoretical foundation of **Eye Movement Desensitization and Reprocessing (EMDR)** therapy, offering a comprehensive explanation for the psychological mechanisms that contribute to the healing process. At its core, the AIP model suggests that the human brain is inherently equipped to process and integrate information related to traumatic or distressing experiences. However, when a person experiences a trauma, this natural processing system can become overloaded, leading to the unprocessed memories being stored in an isolated, fragmented form. These unprocessed memories are believed to be the root cause of a wide range of psychological issues, including anxiety, depression, and post-traumatic stress disorder (PTSD).

According to the AIP model, these unprocessed memories contain the emotions, thoughts, beliefs, and physical sensations that were experienced at the time of the trauma. They are stored in a state that is disconnected from the brain's adaptive learning processes. As a result, these memories can be triggered by current situations that resemble or symbolize aspects of the original trauma, leading to the re-experiencing of the original emotions and sensations. This re-experiencing can occur without an explicit understanding that it is related to the past, causing individuals to react in ways that may seem disproportionate or inappropriate to their current context.

EMDR therapy, grounded in the AIP model, aims to facilitate the accessing and processing of these traumatic memories, allowing for their integration into the larger memory network. Through a structured eight-phase approach that includes the use of bilateral stimulation, EMDR therapy helps to reduce the vividness and emotional charge of the traumatic memories, enabling the brain to resume its natural healing process. The bilateral stimulation, often in the form of guided eye movements, taps, or sounds, is thought to mimic the rapid eye movement (REM) phase of sleep, which is associated with the processing of daily emotional experiences.

The goal of EMDR therapy, as informed by the AIP model, is not to forget the traumatic experiences but to remove their distressing power. By reprocessing these memories, individuals can begin to view the events in a new, less distressing light. This reprocessing allows for a transformation in the emotional, cognitive, and physiological responses associated with the memory. For example, a belief that emerged from a traumatic event such as "I am powerless" can be transformed into a more adaptive and empowering belief like "I am resilient and can handle challenges."

The AIP model also highlights the importance of identifying and targeting specific memories for reprocessing during EMDR therapy. This targeted approach ensures that the therapy addresses the foundational memories contributing to the individual's current difficulties, facilitating a more efficient and effective healing process. By integrating these previously unprocessed memories into the larger memory network, individuals can experience a significant reduction in the symptoms of distress, an increased sense of emotional well-being, and an improved ability to respond adaptively to current and future challenges.

EMDR therapy, through the lens of the AIP model, offers a path to healing that is both structured and adaptive, respecting the unique experiences and needs of each individual. It provides a scientifically grounded, evidence-based approach to addressing the wide range of psychological difficulties that arise from unprocessed traumatic memories, embodying a hopeful message that recovery and emotional freedom are within reach.

4.2: Impact of Unprocessed Memories on Emotions

Unprocessed memories, according to the Adaptive Information Processing (AIP) model, play a significant role in shaping our emotional responses and behaviors in daily life. These memories, encapsulated with the original emotions, thoughts, and physical sensations experienced during traumatic events, remain isolated within the mind's memory system. This isolation prevents the natural processing and integration of these memories into the larger memory network, causing them to be easily triggered by current situations that are reminiscent of the original traumatic event. When triggered, these memories can lead to emotional and physiological responses that are disproportionate to the current situation, often leading to behaviors and decisions that may seem irrational or inappropriate to others.

Emotional Responses:

The emotional impact of unprocessed memories can be profound and varied. Individuals may experience sudden, intense emotions such as fear, anger, sadness, or panic in situations that others might perceive as non-threatening. These emotional responses are the mind's attempt to signal unresolved distress, echoing the unprocessed nature of the traumatic memory. For example, someone with unprocessed memories of abandonment might experience disproportionate anxiety or fear when facing minor separations or changes in their relationships.

Behavioral Patterns:

Behaviors driven by unprocessed memories often serve as coping mechanisms to avoid re-triggering the distress associated with those memories. This can manifest as avoidance behaviors, where individuals steer clear of situations, places, or people that might evoke the traumatic memory. Alternatively, it might result in overcompensation behaviors, such as excessive control or perfectionism, as attempts to prevent perceived threats that resemble past traumas. These patterns are not conscious choices but are driven by the deep-seated need to protect oneself from re-experiencing the pain of the trauma.

Decision Making:

The influence of unprocessed memories extends to decision-making processes. Decisions may be overly influenced by the desire to avoid potential triggers or by the distorted beliefs that have formed around the unprocessed trauma. For instance, someone might avoid pursuing career opportunities for fear of failure, rooted in unprocessed memories of criticism or rejection. The decision-making process becomes constrained by the need to minimize distress, often at the expense of personal growth and fulfillment.

Physical Sensations:

Unprocessed memories can also manifest through physical sensations or symptoms when triggered. These might include heart palpitations, sweating, trembling, or other stress-related physical reactions. These sensations are the body's response to the perceived threat, a remnant of the fight-or-flight response initially experienced during the traumatic event.

To address the impact of unprocessed memories on emotions, behaviors, and decision-making, EMDR therapy facilitates the processing and integration of these memories into the larger memory network. Through the use of bilateral stimulation, EMDR therapy helps to reduce the vividness and emotional charge of the traumatic memories, enabling individuals to view the events in a new, less distressing light. This process allows for the transformation of the emotional, cognitive, and physiological responses associated with the memory, leading to more adaptive behaviors, healthier decision-making, and a reduction in distressing physical sensations. By reprocessing these memories, individuals can break free from the constraints imposed by unprocessed trauma, opening the door to a more adaptive and fulfilling engagement with life.

4.3: The Brain's Reprocessing for Healing

The human brain possesses a remarkable capacity for healing and adaptation, particularly when it comes to processing traumatic memories. At the heart of Eye Movement Desensitization and Reprocessing (EMDR) therapy is the understanding that the brain can heal from psychological trauma much like the body recovers from physical trauma. When you cut your finger, your body works to close the wound. If a foreign object or repeated injury irritates the wound, it festers and does not heal. Similarly, current methods of processing traumatic memories can leave the emotional wound unhealed, and the memory can continue to cause pain. This is where the brain's need for reprocessing becomes crucial.

Reprocessing in the context of EMDR involves the activation of the brain's inherent ability to move toward mental health. EMDR facilitates this process by targeting the unprocessed memories that contain the negative emotions, sensations, and beliefs. By engaging the brain's adaptive information processing system, EMDR therapy helps the mind metabolize these stuck memories, allowing for the transformation of pain into a state of emotional learning and growth.

The process begins with the identification of a target memory. The therapist then guides the individual through a series of bilateral stimulations, such as eye movements or taps. This external stimulus plays a key role in the reprocessing phase, as it appears to jumpstart the brain's natural healing process. It's akin to the brain engaging in a deep, restorative sleep, but while the individual is awake, allowing for the conscious processing of traumatic memories.

Bilateral stimulation is believed to mimic the psychological state that occurs during Rapid Eye Movement (REM) sleep. During REM sleep, the brain processes the day's emotional experiences. EMDR's use of similar bilateral movements facilitates the connection between the brain's two hemispheres, promoting the integration of traumatic memories into the general memory system. This integration is critical for healing, as it transforms the memory from a present, distressing experience into a past event that no longer has the same emotional power over the individual.

The reprocessing phase is not about erasing the memory. Instead, it's about altering the emotional response associated with the memory. Before treatment, the memory might trigger intense fear, sadness, or anger. After successful EMDR therapy, the memory will likely still be recognized as unpleasant or even deeply distressing, but it will no longer hold the same power to upset or harm the individual's emotional well-being.

Positive cognitive shifts are another significant outcome of the reprocessing phase. As the emotional charge of the memory diminishes, negative beliefs about oneself related to the trauma ("I am powerless," "I am unworthy") can shift to more positive and empowering beliefs ("I am resilient," "I am worthy of love and happiness"). This cognitive shift is crucial for the individual's emotional healing and personal growth, as it reflects an internalization of the trauma's lessons without the continued suffering.

In essence, the brain's need for reprocessing to heal underscores the transformative potential of EMDR therapy. By harnessing the brain's natural healing processes, individuals can move through and beyond their trauma, achieving a state of emotional freedom that once seemed out of reach. This capacity for healing is not just a testament to the resilience of the human spirit but also to the intricate and profound mechanisms of the human brain.

Chapter 5: EMDR for Serious Mental Health Issues

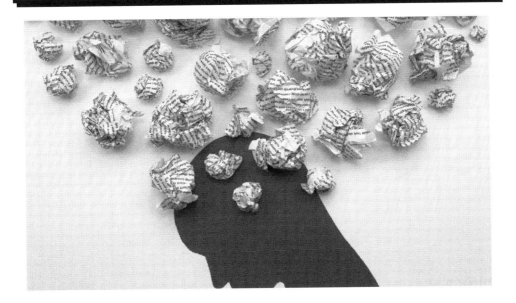

5.1: When and Why to Consult a Specialist

Recognizing the need to consult a specialist for EMDR therapy is a crucial step in addressing complex mental health issues. This therapy, while profoundly transformative, requires professional guidance to navigate the intricacies of serious conditions. There are several scenarios where seeking a specialist's expertise becomes not just beneficial but essential.

Complex Trauma and PTSD:

When an individual is grappling with the aftermath of severe trauma or Post-Traumatic Stress Disorder, the layers of emotional and psychological distress can be deep-rooted. A specialist in EMDR is trained to carefully unravel these layers, providing a structured and safe approach to trauma processing that a general therapist might not offer.

Persistent Anxiety and Depression:

While mild forms of anxiety and depression might be alleviated through self-help techniques, chronic cases often necessitate a specialist's intervention. EMDR therapists can identify and target the specific memories and beliefs fueling these conditions, promoting a more profound and lasting healing process.

Dissociative Disorders:

These disorders represent a complex challenge that requires a nuanced understanding of the human psyche. Specialists in EMDR possess the skills to create a therapeutic plan that addresses the unique ways dissociation can affect memory and identity, ensuring that therapy is both effective and grounded in safety.

Addiction and Substance Abuse:

The roots of addiction often lie in unresolved trauma and emotional pain. An EMDR specialist can work to uncover and process these underlying issues, offering a path to recovery that addresses both the symptoms and the cause.

Severe Phobias:

When phobias significantly impact an individual's ability to function in daily life, specialized EMDR therapy can offer a targeted approach to desensitization and reprocessing, providing relief from the intense and often debilitating fear.

In each of these cases, the specialized training and experience of an EMDR therapist are invaluable. They can offer a tailored therapeutic approach that addresses the complexity of the condition, supports the individual's unique healing journey, and fosters a safe environment for emotional and psychological growth. Consulting with a specialist ensures that the therapy is not only effective but also aligns with the individual's specific needs and therapy goals.

5.2: Serious Conditions EMDR Can Address

5.2.1: EMDR for PTSD: Reducing Traumatic Symptoms

Eye Movement Desensitization and Reprocessing (EMDR) therapy offers a transformative approach for individuals grappling with Post-Traumatic Stress Disorder (PTSD). This condition, characterized by intense and distressing memories of traumatic events, often manifests through debilitating symptoms such as **flashbacks**, **nightmares**, and **hypervigilance**. The core of EMDR therapy lies in its ability to facilitate the processing of these traumatic memories, aiming to reduce their hold on the individual's emotional well-being.

The process begins with the identification of specific traumatic memories that serve as the foundation for PTSD symptoms. Through a structured protocol, EMDR therapy engages the brain's innate healing capabilities using **bilateral stimulation**—a key component that involves guided eye movements, taps, or tones. This stimulation is thought to mimic the psychological state associated with Rapid Eye Movement (REM) sleep, a phase crucial for processing daily emotional experiences.

During EMDR sessions, individuals are guided to briefly focus on the traumatic memory while simultaneously experiencing bilateral stimulation. This dual attention facilitates the reprocessing of the memory, aiming to alter its emotional impact. Essentially, the goal is not to erase the memory but to transform the way it is stored in the brain—reducing its intensity and the distress associated with it.

As the traumatic memory is reprocessed, the symptoms of PTSD, such as **flashbacks** and **nightmares**, begin to diminish. EMDR therapy helps dissociate the emotional charge from the memory itself, allowing individuals to recall their experiences without the overwhelming emotional response previously elicited. This decrease in symptom severity is a critical step toward regaining a sense of control and safety.

Hypervigilance, another hallmark of PTSD, is addressed through EMDR by working on the individual's heightened state of alertness to perceived threats. By reprocessing the memories that contribute to this constant state of alert, individuals can experience a reduction in anxiety and an increased sense of security in their environment.

29

EMDR therapy's effectiveness in treating PTSD is supported by numerous studies, highlighting its capacity to provide relief even when other treatments have been unsuccessful. It is a preferred method for many because it can achieve results without the need for detailed verbal recounting of the traumatic event, thereby reducing the risk of re-traumatization.

For those seeking relief from the symptoms of PTSD, EMDR therapy represents a hopeful pathway to recovery. It offers a scientifically backed, structured approach to healing that honors the brain's natural processing abilities. By directly addressing the root cause of PTSD symptoms—the unprocessed traumatic memories—EMDR therapy facilitates emotional healing and fosters a renewed sense of empowerment.

5.2.2: EMDR and Complex PTSD Healing

Complex PTSD, or C-PTSD, arises from enduring traumatic circumstances over an extended period, often characterized by a lack of control and the impossibility of escape. Unlike singular traumatic events that lead to PTSD, C-PTSD stems from chronic exposure to stressors, leading to profound and multifaceted impacts on an individual's emotional regulation and self-perception. Eye Movement Desensitization and Reprocessing (EMDR) therapy has emerged as a potent tool in addressing the deep-seated effects of such prolonged trauma, offering a pathway to healing that is both structured and empathetic.

The core of EMDR's effectiveness in treating C-PTSD lies in its unique approach to processing distressing memories. Through bilateral stimulation, typically involving guided eye movements, EMDR facilitates the brain's natural healing processes, allowing individuals to reprocess traumatic memories in a way that diminishes their emotional intensity. This reprocessing is crucial for individuals with C-PTSD, as it aids in detangling the complex web of memories that contribute to ongoing emotional dysregulation and negative self-conception.

For those grappling with **C-PTSD**, emotional regulation is often a significant challenge. The chronic nature of their trauma can lead to persistent feelings of sadness, anger, fear, or numbness, making it difficult to respond to everyday situations in a balanced and measured way. EMDR therapy addresses this by helping individuals to process the underlying traumatic memories that fuel these intense emotional responses. As these memories are reprocessed, individuals often find that their emotional reactions become less overwhelming, making it easier to engage in effective emotional regulation.

Moreover, C-PTSD can profoundly affect an individual's perception of themselves, often leading to a deeply ingrained sense of worthlessness or inadequacy. This negative self-concept is reinforced by the traumatic memories and the ongoing distress they cause. EMDR therapy, through its phased approach and focus on positive belief installation, offers an opportunity to challenge and reframe these negative self-beliefs. As traumatic memories are processed and the emotional charge they carry is reduced, individuals are guided to incorporate new, positive beliefs about themselves. This shift is pivotal, as it fosters a more compassionate and empowering self-view.

The therapeutic journey with EMDR for those affected by C-PTSD is not just about managing symptoms but about fostering a profound transformation in how they relate to themselves and their past experiences. By addressing the roots of emotional dysregulation and negative self-perception, EMDR paves the way for individuals to reclaim a sense of control over their lives. This sense of empowerment is a critical component of healing from C-PTSD, as it counteracts feelings of helplessness and fosters resilience.

In essence, EMDR's contribution to healing from C-PTSD extends beyond symptom relief, offering a comprehensive approach that addresses the multifaceted impacts of chronic trauma. Through the strategic reprocessing of traumatic memories, individuals can achieve significant improvements in emotional regulation and embark on a journey toward a more positive and grounded sense of self. This transformative process underscores the potential of EMDR therapy to provide not just relief but a pathway to reclaiming one's life from the shadows of prolonged trauma.

5.2.3: EMDR for Reducing Anxiety Disorders

Anxiety disorders encompass a range of conditions characterized by excessive fear and anxiety that can significantly impact an individual's daily life. These conditions include generalized anxiety disorder, where individuals experience persistent worry about various events or activities, and social anxiety disorder, characterized by intense fear of social situations due to concerns about being judged or embarrassed. Eye Movement Desensitization and Reprocessing (EMDR) therapy has been recognized for its efficacy in addressing the root causes of these anxiety disorders by targeting the distressing memories and experiences that fuel them.

At the core of EMDR's approach to treating anxiety disorders is the Adaptive Information Processing (AIP) model, which posits that psychological stress and disorders stem from unprocessed memories of disturbing events. These unprocessed memories contain the emotions, thoughts, beliefs, and physical sensations experienced at the time of the event, which can be triggered by current situations, leading to anxiety responses. EMDR therapy facilitates the processing of these memories, aiming to desensitize the individual to the distressing emotions associated with them and reframe negative beliefs into positive ones.

The process begins with the therapist working with the individual to identify specific memories contributing to their anxiety. Once these memories are pinpointed, EMDR uses bilateral stimulation, such as guided eye movements, to activate the brain's information processing system, allowing these memories to be reprocessed. During this phase, individuals may experience the emergence of new insights, emotions, or memories related to the original event, which are then further processed until the emotional charge is significantly reduced or eliminated.

This reprocessing is crucial for individuals with anxiety disorders, as it helps to diminish the physiological arousal associated with the triggering memories, thereby reducing symptoms of anxiety. For example, someone with social anxiety might have underlying memories of embarrassing or humiliating experiences. Through EMDR, these memories can be reprocessed, reducing the intense fear and avoidance behavior associated with social situations. Similarly, individuals with generalized anxiety disorder may find that EMDR helps to alleviate the pervasive worry and physical symptoms of anxiety by addressing the past experiences that underlie their excessive concerns about future events.

32

EMDR therapy offers a structured yet flexible approach to anxiety disorders, allowing individuals to work through their distressing memories at their own pace. The therapist's role is to guide and support the individual through this process, ensuring a safe and therapeutic environment. As the therapy progresses, individuals often report a decrease in anxiety symptoms, an increase in emotional stability, and a greater sense of control over their reactions to situations that previously triggered their anxiety.

Through the lens of the AIP model, EMDR therapy not only targets the symptoms of anxiety but also aims to fundamentally alter the way distressing memories are stored in the brain. This alteration is believed to reduce the likelihood of these memories triggering anxiety responses in the future. As individuals progress through EMDR sessions, they often report a newfound ability to approach situations that would have previously provoked anxiety with a sense of calmness and confidence. This shift can be particularly empowering for those who have felt constrained by their anxiety, opening up new possibilities for engagement in personal, social, and professional realms.

Moreover, the benefits of EMDR in treating anxiety disorders extend beyond symptom reduction. Many individuals experience improvements in self-esteem and overall well-being as they process and move beyond the memories that have fueled their anxiety. This holistic approach to healing is a key aspect of EMDR therapy, reflecting its potential to facilitate profound personal transformation and growth.

In addition to direct treatment of anxiety symptoms, EMDR therapy also incorporates techniques for managing future stressors and triggers. Individuals learn coping strategies and resilience-building skills that can help them navigate life's challenges more effectively. This proactive component of EMDR ensures that the benefits of therapy are sustainable, equipping individuals with the tools they need to maintain their emotional balance long after therapy has concluded.

The success of EMDR in treating anxiety disorders is supported by a growing body of research, which highlights its effectiveness across a range of anxiety-related conditions. It's worth noting that while EMDR is a powerful therapeutic tool, its success depends on the individual's readiness for therapy, the skill of the therapist, and the complexity of the anxiety disorder being treated. Therefore, a collaborative approach between the individual and therapist, grounded in mutual trust and commitment to the therapeutic process, is crucial for achieving the best outcomes.

In conclusion, **EMDR therapy offers a promising avenue for individuals seeking relief from anxiety disorders**. By addressing the root causes of anxiety through the reprocessing of distressing memories, EMDR facilitates a shift towards emotional freedom and resilience. With the guidance of a skilled therapist, individuals can embark on a transformative journey, moving beyond the constraints of anxiety to lead richer, more fulfilling lives.

5.2.4: EMDR for Depression Transformation

Depression, a condition often characterized by persistent sadness, loss of interest in activities, and a profound sense of despair, can deeply affect an individual's quality of life. The roots of depression are complex and multifaceted, involving a combination of biological, psychological, and social factors. Among these, painful memories and unresolved emotional issues can significantly contribute to the condition's severity and persistence. Eye Movement Desensitization and Reprocessing (EMDR) therapy emerges as a powerful intervention, targeting the distressing memories that may fuel depressive episodes, facilitating a process of healing and positive change.

The essence of EMDR's application in treating depression lies in its structured approach to identifying and processing the distressing memories that contribute to the depressive state. This therapeutic process begins with the establishment of a safe and trusting therapeutic environment, where individuals feel supported in confronting their painful memories. The therapist guides the individual through a series of phases designed to desensitize the emotional impact of these memories and reprocess them in a way that reduces their negative influence on the individual's emotional well-being.

During the desensitization phase, the individual is asked to focus on a specific distressing memory while simultaneously engaging in bilateral stimulation, such as guided eye movements or taps. This dual attention facilitates the brain's natural healing processes, allowing for the reprocessing of the memory. It's hypothesized that this process mimics the psychological state associated with Rapid Eye Movement (REM) sleep, during which the brain organizes and integrates memories and emotions. Through this reprocessing, the painful memory's emotional charge is diminished, altering its impact on the individual's mood and overall mental state.

The installation of positive beliefs plays a critical role in EMDR therapy for depression. As the distressing memories are reprocessed, they are replaced with positive cognitions and beliefs about the self. For instance, a memory that previously evoked feelings of worthlessness or guilt may be transformed to reinforce a sense of self-worth and forgiveness. This shift is crucial in alleviating depressive symptoms, as it directly counters the negative self-perceptions and beliefs that often accompany and exacerbate depression.

EMDR therapy also addresses the physiological symptoms of depression. The body scan phase of EMDR allows individuals to identify and release any physical tension or discomfort associated with their distressing memories. This step is significant, as depression often manifests physically, through changes in energy levels, sleep patterns, and overall physical health. By connecting the mind and body in the healing process, EMDR supports a more holistic approach to overcoming depression.

The closure and reevaluation phases ensure that the therapeutic gains are consolidated and that the individual has strategies to maintain their emotional equilibrium following therapy. These steps are vital in providing a sense of closure and achievement, reinforcing the individual's capacity to manage their emotional state effectively.

For individuals grappling with depression, EMDR therapy offers a hopeful path forward. By directly addressing the painful memories and unresolved issues contributing to their condition, EMDR facilitates a process of emotional healing and transformation. This therapy not only aims to alleviate the symptoms of depression but also empowers individuals to reclaim their lives, fostering resilience and a renewed sense of purpose. Through the strategic reprocessing of distressing memories, EMDR therapy can significantly impact those seeking to overcome depression, promoting lasting change and emotional freedom.

5.2.5: EMDR for Phobia Desensitization

Phobias, defined as intense and irrational fears of specific objects, situations, or activities, can severely limit an individual's daily functioning and overall quality of life. These profound fears trigger a cascade of physical and emotional responses, including panic attacks, rapid heartbeat, and overwhelming anxiety, at the mere anticipation or presence of the feared object or situation. The mechanism behind phobias involves the brain's maladaptive encoding of fear responses to harmless stimuli, turning them into triggers that elicit disproportionate reactions. Eye Movement Desensitization and Reprocessing (EMDR) therapy, with its unique approach to processing distressing memories and experiences, offers a promising avenue for desensitizing these triggers, thereby mitigating the phobic response and improving emotional well-being.

At the heart of EMDR's application to phobia treatment is the Adaptive Information Processing (AIP) model, which posits that psychological distress, including phobias, stems from unprocessed memories and experiences. These unprocessed memories, loaded with the original emotional and physiological distress, are believed to be the foundation of the phobic response. EMDR therapy aims to access these memories and facilitate their processing, transforming the stored distressing memories into neutral or less distressing ones. This process effectively reduces the emotional and physiological responses previously associated with the phobic stimulus.

The EMDR treatment for phobias typically begins with the identification of the memory or memories linked to the onset of the phobia. This phase is crucial as it targets the root cause of the phobia rather than just its symptoms. Following this, the therapist guides the individual through a series of bilateral stimulations, such as side-to-side eye movements, taps, or tones, while the individual focuses on aspects of the phobia. This bilateral stimulation is a core component of EMDR and is thought to facilitate the brain's natural healing process, akin to the processing that occurs during REM sleep. Through this process, the emotional charge associated with the phobic memory is reduced, leading to a decrease in the phobic reaction.

An essential aspect of EMDR therapy for phobias is the installation of positive beliefs. For instance, a person with a fear of flying might replace the belief "I am not safe on an airplane" with "I can manage my fear and feel calm while flying." This step is not about convincing the individual that the phobic object or situation is entirely harmless but about fostering a sense of control and safety when confronted with it.

EMDR therapy also incorporates techniques for managing physiological arousal and anxiety, teaching individuals grounding and relaxation strategies that can be used in anticipation of or during exposure to the phobic stimulus. These strategies are vital for empowering the individual to face the feared object or situation with reduced anxiety, facilitating a gradual desensitization to the phobia.

Moreover, EMDR's structured yet flexible approach allows for the therapy to be tailored to the individual's specific phobia and response pattern. This personalized approach ensures that the therapy addresses the unique aspects of each person's phobia, enhancing its effectiveness. As the feared objects or situations are reprocessed and the associated distress is alleviated, individuals often experience a significant improvement in their ability to engage in activities they had been avoiding, leading to an enhanced quality of life.

The success of EMDR in treating phobias is supported by its focus on altering the dysfunctional encoding of fear responses in the brain. By reprocessing the distressing memories that underlie the phobia, EMDR therapy reduces the pathological fear response, allowing individuals to approach previously feared situations with a new sense of confidence and emotional freedom. This therapeutic process not only addresses the symptoms of the phobia but also contributes to the individual's overall emotional resilience, empowering them to face future challenges with greater ease. Through the strategic application of EMDR therapy, individuals with phobias can achieve a significant reduction in their fear and anxiety, opening the door to a life no longer constrained by irrational fears.

5.2.6: EMDR for Addiction Recovery

In addressing addictions, Eye Movement Desensitization and Reprocessing (EMDR) therapy presents a groundbreaking approach that goes beyond mere symptom management to target the root causes of dependency behaviors. This method is particularly effective in identifying and reprocessing the traumatic memories and emotional pain that often underlie addictive patterns, thereby reducing the intense cravings that drive substance use and other compulsive behaviors.

The process begins with the identification of traumatic or distressing experiences that may not be initially apparent to the individual suffering from addiction. These experiences, whether they are acute, like a singular traumatic event, or chronic, such as ongoing emotional neglect in childhood, contribute to the development of maladaptive coping mechanisms, including substance abuse. The therapist works with the individual to pinpoint these key memories for targeted reprocessing.

EMDR therapy employs bilateral stimulation, typically through guided eye movements, to facilitate the brain's natural healing process. This stimulation is thought to mimic the psychological state associated with Rapid Eye Movement (REM) sleep, a phase of sleep that is crucial for processing emotional experiences. By activating both hemispheres of the brain, EMDR helps to desensitize the individual to the emotional impact of these memories, effectively reducing their influence on the individual's current emotional state and behavior.

As these memories are processed, the therapy simultaneously works to instill positive beliefs and coping mechanisms. Where once the memory of a traumatic event might have led to feelings of worthlessness and a subsequent need to numb those feelings with substances, the individual can begin to associate that memory with a sense of resilience and self-worth. This shift is crucial in reducing cravings, as the individual no longer feels a compelling need to escape their emotions through addictive behaviors.

Moreover, EMDR therapy addresses the physiological aspect of addiction. The bilateral stimulation used in EMDR can help to regulate the nervous system, reducing the heightened stress response that often accompanies and exacerbates cravings. By bringing the body back into a state of equilibrium, individuals are better equipped to manage stress without resorting to substance use.

This holistic approach to treating addiction with EMDR does not solely focus on the addiction itself but rather views it as a symptom of underlying trauma and unprocessed emotional pain. Through the reprocessing of these foundational experiences, individuals can achieve a profound and lasting recovery that goes beyond abstinence to encompass a fuller sense of emotional freedom and well-being.

EMDR therapy, therefore, offers a powerful tool in the arsenal against addiction, providing hope and a pathway to healing for those trapped in the cycle of dependency. Its effectiveness lies in its ability to unearth and address the deep-seated emotional triggers of addiction, paving the way for genuine and sustainable change.

5.3: EMDR and Collaborative Professional Support

Integrating Eye Movement Desensitization and Reprocessing (EMDR) into a broader therapeutic framework significantly enhances the support available to individuals dealing with complex psychological issues. This integration underscores the importance of a collaborative approach between the client and mental health professionals, ensuring that EMDR therapy is not viewed in isolation but as part of a comprehensive treatment plan. The synergy between EMDR and other therapeutic modalities offers a multifaceted approach to healing, addressing various dimensions of mental health with the flexibility to tailor interventions to the unique needs of each individual.

Collaborative Treatment Planning:

The initial phase involves developing a treatment plan that incorporates EMDR alongside other therapeutic techniques. This plan is crafted through a collaborative process, involving input from both the client and the therapist. The objective is to identify specific goals and outcomes, ensuring that the chosen strategies align with the client's needs, preferences, and readiness for EMDR therapy.

Complementary Therapies:

EMDR can be effectively combined with cognitive-behavioral therapy (CBT), dialectical behavior therapy (DBT), and other evidence-based practices. For instance, CBT can provide clients with tools for managing distressing thoughts and behaviors, while EMDR focuses on processing and integrating traumatic memories. This combination allows for a more comprehensive approach to treatment, addressing both current symptoms and underlying trauma.

Multidisciplinary Support:

In cases involving severe mental health issues, a multidisciplinary team approach can be beneficial. This team may include psychiatrists, clinical psychologists, social workers, and other specialists, each contributing their expertise to support the client's recovery. EMDR therapists work within this team, communicating progress and adjusting their approach based on feedback from other professionals and the client's evolving needs.

Client-Therapist Collaboration:

A key aspect of EMDR's effectiveness lies in the therapeutic alliance between the client and the therapist. This relationship is built on trust, respect, and mutual understanding. The therapist's role is to guide the client through the EMDR process, providing support and encouragement while respecting the client's pace and boundaries. This collaborative dynamic is essential for creating a safe and empowering environment where healing can occur.

Ongoing Assessment and Adjustment:

Treatment effectiveness is continually assessed, with regular check-ins to discuss progress, challenges, and any adjustments needed to the treatment plan. This iterative process ensures that the therapy remains responsive to the client's changing needs, maximizing the benefits of EMDR within the broader therapeutic context.

Educational and Supportive Interventions:

Part of the collaborative work also involves educating clients about stress management, coping strategies, and the importance of self-care. These interventions complement the EMDR process, equipping clients with the skills needed to maintain their well-being beyond the therapy sessions.

Professional Development and Consultation:

Therapists often engage in ongoing professional development and consultation with peers to enhance their understanding of EMDR and its integration with other therapies. This commitment to learning ensures that clients receive the most effective, evidence-based care possible.

The integration of EMDR with professional support exemplifies a holistic approach to mental health care. It acknowledges the complexity of human psychology and the need for diverse therapeutic strategies to address the multifaceted nature of psychological distress. Through collaborative planning, complementary therapies, and a strong therapeutic alliance, EMDR becomes a powerful tool in the journey toward healing and emotional freedom.

Chapter 6: The Eight Phases of EMDR Therapy

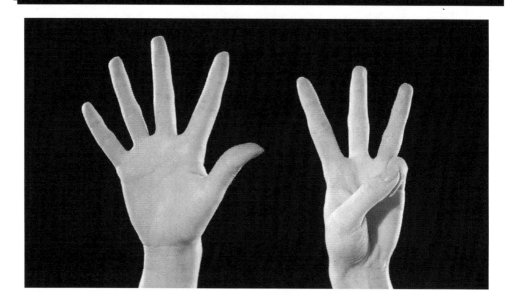

6.1: History Taking and Treatment Planning

The initial stage of Eye Movement Desensitization and Reprocessing therapy, known as **history taking and treatment planning,** is pivotal for laying the foundation of a successful therapeutic journey. This phase is not merely a procedural step but a critical opportunity for the therapist and client to establish a rapport and set the stage for meaningful change. The therapist begins by gathering comprehensive information about the client's life history, including any significant events, challenges, and the specific issues they wish to address through EMDR. This detailed exploration serves multiple purposes. Firstly, it allows the therapist to identify potential targets for reprocessing, including past traumas, present challenges, and future concerns that may be contributing to the client's psychological distress. These targets are not chosen at random but are carefully selected based on their relevance and impact on the client's current well-being.

Moreover, this phase is instrumental in developing a tailored treatment plan that aligns with the client's unique needs and therapeutic goals. By understanding the client's background, the therapist can prioritize which memories or experiences to address first, considering both the potential for emotional intensity and the readiness of the client to engage in the reprocessing work. The treatment plan is a dynamic document, subject to revision as therapy progresses and new insights emerge. It acts as a roadmap, guiding the therapeutic process while allowing for flexibility to adapt to the client's evolving needs.

Another critical aspect of this phase is the assessment of the client's current coping mechanisms and resources. The therapist evaluates the client's psychological strengths and vulnerabilities to ensure they are adequately prepared for the emotional work ahead. This evaluation may lead to the incorporation of additional preparatory steps, such as strengthening the client's grounding techniques or establishing a robust support system, before proceeding with the more intensive aspects of EMDR therapy.

The collaborative nature of history taking and treatment planning cannot be overstated. It is a process that requires active participation from the client, fostering a sense of agency and partnership in their healing journey. This collaboration also helps to build trust between the client and therapist, a crucial element for the therapeutic alliance and the overall success of the therapy.

The initial phase of history taking and treatment planning is a cornerstone of EMDR therapy. It sets the direction for the therapeutic journey, ensuring that the therapy is personalized, goal-oriented, and grounded in the client's lived experience. By meticulously gathering and analyzing the client's history, the therapist can identify the most salient targets for reprocessing, tailor the treatment plan to the client's specific needs, and prepare the client for the transformative work of EMDR therapy. This careful preparation and planning are what make EMDR a powerful tool for healing and change, allowing individuals to process and overcome their past traumas and move forward with greater emotional freedom and resilience.

6.2: Preparation and Creating a Safe Space

Creating a safe space is foundational in the EMDR therapy process, serving as a secure base from which individuals can explore and reprocess traumatic memories without fear of retraumatization. This phase is crucial for building trust between the therapist and the client, ensuring that the client feels supported and safe throughout their therapeutic journey. The concept of a safe space is not merely physical but also psychological, encompassing an environment where clients can express themselves freely, without judgment, and with the assurance of confidentiality and understanding.

Establishing Trust:

The therapeutic relationship is a cornerstone of effective EMDR therapy. From the outset, therapists must communicate their commitment to the client's well-being, emphasizing empathy, respect, and professionalism. This involves clear communication about the therapy process, what the client can expect, and the roles both the therapist and client will play. It's essential for clients to know that they are in control and can pause or stop the process at any point, reinforcing a sense of autonomy and safety.

Introducing EMDR:

For those unfamiliar with EMDR, the concept of reprocessing memories through eye movements or other bilateral stimulation can seem daunting. Therapists should provide a thorough explanation of how EMDR works, including the scientific basis behind it and its proven effectiveness in treating trauma and other psychological stressors. This knowledge helps demystify the process for clients, reducing anxiety and building confidence in the therapy's potential benefits.

Creating a Psychological Safe Space:

Techniques such as guided visualization can be employed to help clients establish a 'safe place' in their mind, a go-to mental refuge they can visualize during or outside of therapy sessions. This mental safe space is a personalized, calm setting where the client feels completely secure and at ease. The therapist guides the client in vividly imagining this place, incorporating all senses to enhance its realness and the comfort it provides. This practice not only aids in managing distress during sessions but also equips clients with a valuable tool for self-soothing in their daily lives.

Grounding Techniques:

Before delving into trauma work, it's vital that clients are equipped with grounding techniques to help them manage emotional distress. These can include focused breathing, mindfulness exercises, and physical grounding methods like holding a textured object. Such techniques help clients stay present and connected to the here and now, providing a counterbalance to the intense emotions that can arise during memory reprocessing.

Ensuring Physical Comfort:

The physical environment where therapy takes place should be conducive to relaxation and concentration. This means a quiet, private space where interruptions are minimized. Comfortable seating, appropriate lighting, and a temperature-controlled room all contribute to a sense of safety and calm. The therapist might also offer adjustments to the space based on the client's preferences, further personalizing the therapeutic environment.

Gradual Exposure:

Particularly in the early stages of therapy, it's important that exposure to traumatic memories is approached gradually, with the therapist guiding the client in titrating their exposure to distressing content. This careful pacing ensures that the client does not become overwhelmed and that the sense of safety within the therapeutic space is maintained.

Reinforcing the Safe Space at Each Session:

At the beginning of subsequent sessions, revisiting and reinforcing the concept of the safe space helps to re-establish the secure base before any therapeutic work begins. The therapist may ask the client to briefly engage with their mental safe place or use grounding techniques, thereby starting each session from a place of stability.

In summary, the preparation phase and the creation of a safe space are integral to the success of EMDR therapy. They lay the groundwork for a therapeutic alliance based on trust, safety, and mutual respect, enabling clients to engage in the challenging work of processing and healing from trauma. Through careful explanation, the establishment of a psychological safe haven, and the use of grounding techniques, therapists can help clients feel empowered and supported as they embark on their journey towards recovery.

6.3: Assessing Triggers and Emotions

In the third phase of EMDR therapy, the focus shifts to **assessing triggers and emotions**, a critical step that involves delving into the client's internal landscape to identify the specific images, emotions, and negative beliefs tied to traumatic memories. This process is intricate, requiring the therapist and client to work closely together to unearth the roots of distress that may not be immediately apparent. The therapist employs a structured approach to guide the client through this exploration, using targeted questions and observation to pinpoint the exact nature of the triggers.

Identifying Triggers:

The first step involves recognizing the external situations or internal thoughts that elicit a strong emotional response. Triggers can be as varied as a particular sound, a specific place, or even a certain type of interaction with others. The therapist helps the client to map these triggers, noting how each one is connected to specific memories or feelings. This mapping is essential for understanding the client's unique response patterns and preparing for the desensitization phase of EMDR.

Exploring Emotions:

Once triggers are identified, the therapist encourages the client to explore the emotions associated with each trigger. This exploration is not about reliving the trauma but rather acknowledging the feelings that arise when thinking about it. Common emotions might include fear, sadness, anger, or shame. The therapist supports the client in naming these emotions, which is a powerful step towards processing and integrating the traumatic experience.

Uncovering Negative Beliefs:

Traumatic memories often lead to the formation of negative beliefs about oneself, such as "I am powerless" or "I am unworthy." These beliefs are deeply ingrained and can influence the client's behavior and interactions with the world. The therapist guides the client to articulate these beliefs, linking them to the identified triggers and emotions. Understanding these negative beliefs is pivotal for the next phase of EMDR, where the goal is to replace them with positive, empowering beliefs.

Techniques Used in This Phase:

To facilitate this assessment, the therapist might use various techniques, including:

- **Socratic Questioning**: Asking open-ended questions that encourage the client to reflect on their experiences and the meanings they've attached to them.

- **Imagery**: Encouraging the client to visualize the triggering event or situation and describe the images that come to mind. This technique helps in identifying the sensory details associated with the memory, which might be overlooked but are crucial for the reprocessing stage.

- **Emotion Tracking**: Teaching the client to track their emotional responses as they discuss the triggers, which helps in recognizing patterns and intensities of feelings.

Throughout this phase, the therapist maintains a supportive and empathetic stance, ensuring the client feels safe and understood. The aim is not only to identify triggers, emotions, and beliefs but also to start laying the groundwork for transforming these elements through the therapeutic process. This phase is foundational, setting the stage for the more active reprocessing work that follows in EMDR therapy. It requires patience and sensitivity, as clients may find it challenging to articulate their experiences and emotions. However, this detailed assessment is crucial for effective therapy, as it ensures that the subsequent phases are tailored to the client's specific needs and experiences, ultimately facilitating healing and recovery.

6.4: Desensitization and Memory Reprocessing

Moving into the desensitization and memory reprocessing phase, this segment of therapy is where the core of EMDR's transformative power lies. The process is designed to diminish the emotional intensity associated with distressing memories, making them less overwhelming for the individual. This is achieved through **bilateral stimulation**, a distinctive feature of EMDR therapy that involves guiding the client to focus on a traumatic memory while simultaneously experiencing bilateral sensory input, such as side-to-side eye movements, auditory tones, or tactile taps.

The bilateral stimulation is thought to facilitate the brain's information processing system, allowing for the distressing memory to be integrated into the larger narrative of the individual's life without the intense emotional charge that was previously attached to it. It mirrors the natural healing process that occurs during REM sleep, where the brain processes daily emotional experiences. The goal is to help the client reprocess the traumatic memory in a way that it no longer triggers debilitating emotional responses.

Steps in the Desensitization and Memory Reprocessing Phase:

1. Identification of Target Memory: The therapist and client collaborate to select a specific traumatic memory to target. This memory is usually one that is vivid and distressing and is associated with negative beliefs about oneself.

2. Activation of the Memory: The client is asked to bring the memory to mind, including the associated images, thoughts, emotions, and bodily sensations. This activation prepares the brain for the reprocessing work.

3. Application of Bilateral Stimulation: While focusing on the target memory, the client is exposed to bilateral stimulation. The therapist may use various methods, such as guiding the client's eyes to move back and forth, playing sounds that alternate between the left and right ear, or tapping on the client's hands.

4. Processing of the Memory: As the bilateral stimulation occurs, the client simply notices whatever spontaneously happens in their mind without trying to control or judge the experience. This might include changes in the memory images, shifts in emotions, or new insights.

5. Installation of Positive Beliefs: Once the distressing memory has been processed and the emotional charge reduced, the therapist helps the client to connect the memory with positive beliefs about themselves. For example, a belief such as "I am powerless" might be replaced with "I am resilient".

6. Body Scan: The client is then asked to think about the original memory while scanning their body for any residual tension or uncomfortable sensations. If any are found, these sensations are targeted with further bilateral stimulation until the client feels at ease.

The pace of this phase is carefully managed by the therapist, ensuring that the client remains within their window of tolerance for emotional distress. It's a process that requires patience and may need to be revisited across multiple sessions for a single memory or set of related memories.

The effectiveness of this phase hinges on the client's ability to stay present with the traumatic memory while simultaneously engaging with the bilateral stimulation. It's a unique balancing act that allows the brain to process and integrate traumatic experiences in a way that reduces their power to cause current distress.

By the end of the desensitization and memory reprocessing phase, clients often report a significant reduction in the emotional intensity of the memory. They may find that recalling the memory no longer brings up the strong negative emotions it once did, or that they can now think about the memory with a sense of detachment or neutrality. This phase is a pivotal moment in the journey towards healing, marking a turning point where the grip of past traumas begins to loosen, allowing for a new sense of freedom and emotional well-being.

6.5: Installing Positive Beliefs

In Phase 5 of EMDR therapy, the focus shifts significantly towards the reinforcement of positive beliefs, a crucial step that facilitates profound personal transformation. This stage is designed to replace the negative cognitions that have been identified and processed in the earlier phases with empowering, affirmative beliefs. The process is not merely about negating the old beliefs but about instilling new ones that support the individual's growth and emotional freedom.

The therapist begins by collaborating with the individual to identify specific positive beliefs that are both realistic and relevant to the person's goals and aspirations. These beliefs should directly counter the negative self-perceptions that were linked to the traumatic memories. For instance, if a person has been harboring the belief "I am powerless," a suitable positive belief to install might be "I have the power to effect change in my life."

Bilateral stimulation is once again employed during this phase, but this time it serves to reinforce the newly identified positive beliefs. The individual focuses on the positive cognition while simultaneously engaging in bilateral stimulation, which helps to integrate this belief into their cognitive framework. The sensation is akin to "sealing in" the positive belief, making it a part of the individual's core understanding of themselves and their capabilities.

It is essential for the therapist to gauge the individual's **"validity of cognition" (VOC) scale**, which measures how true the positive belief feels on a scale from 1 to 7. The goal is to reach a VOC as close to 7 as possible, indicating that the individual genuinely believes in the positive cognition. The therapist and individual work together, using repeated rounds of bilateral stimulation, until the desired level of belief in the positive cognition is achieved.

This phase is not just about believing in positive statements but about embodying them. Individuals are encouraged to recall instances from their past, however minor, that demonstrate the positive belief in action. This exercise helps to solidify the belief by providing evidence from the individual's own life experiences that support the new, positive cognition.

Moreover, therapists often integrate **future template work** during this phase. This involves the individual visualizing themselves in future scenarios where they successfully apply this new belief, further reinforcing its validity and the individual's ability to live by this positive cognition in real-life situations.

The successful installation of positive beliefs is a transformative moment in EMDR therapy. It marks a shift from being anchored by past traumas to moving forward with a strengthened sense of self and a more optimistic outlook on life. This phase is critical in empowering individuals to rewrite their narrative, not defined by trauma but by resilience, strength, and the capacity for growth and change.

6.6: Body Scan: Connecting Mind and Body

The body scan phase is a pivotal moment in EMDR therapy that emphasizes the deep connection between the mind and the body. After the intensive work of identifying, processing, and installing new beliefs, the body scan allows individuals to tune into their physical selves and identify any residual tension or discomfort that might be lingering after the emotional processing. This step is crucial because emotional distress often manifests physically, and unaddressed physical sensations can signal unresolved issues.

During this phase, the therapist guides the individual to mentally scan their body from head to toe, encouraging a mindful awareness of any sensations, no matter how subtle. The person is asked to notice areas of tightness, discomfort, or perhaps numbness, acknowledging these sensations without judgment. This practice is rooted in the understanding that the body holds onto stress and trauma in ways that might not always be conscious or immediately apparent.

The therapist may inquire about the quality of these sensations, asking the individual to describe them in detail - are they sharp, dull, throbbing, hot, or cold? This detailed inquiry helps to bring the individual's full attention to their physical experience, fostering a holistic integration of the therapy's effects.

If areas of tension are identified, the therapist then employs techniques to help release this discomfort. This might involve additional bilateral stimulation, focused breathing exercises, or visualization techniques aimed at relaxing the body and encouraging a flow of energy through areas that had been blocked or constricted. The goal is for the individual to not only cognitively process traumatic memories but to also physically let go of the hold these memories have on their body.

This phase is not a one-time process but can be revisited in subsequent sessions as new layers of emotional processing reveal further physical sensations. It's a testament to the body's role in the healing journey and underscores the importance of addressing both mental and physical aspects of trauma and stress.

The body scan serves as a bridge to the next phase of therapy, ensuring that the individual moves forward without carrying the physical weight of their past experiences. It's a practice that can also be incorporated into daily self-care routines, empowering individuals to maintain a connection with their body's signals and needs beyond the therapy sessions. Through this mindful practice, individuals learn to recognize and respond to their body's wisdom, fostering a deeper healing and a more profound sense of embodiment and presence.

6.7: Closure: Restoring Emotional Balance

The completion of the EMDR session, known as the Closure phase, is crucial for ensuring that individuals leave the therapy space feeling emotionally balanced and grounded. This phase is designed to help individuals transition from the heightened state of emotional processing back to their everyday level of functioning. The therapist plays a key role in guiding this transition in a manner that reinforces the individual's sense of safety and stability. Here are the steps involved in the Closure phase to restore emotional balance:

1. Reorienting to the Present: The therapist assists the individual in becoming fully present in the here and now. This may involve asking the person to open their eyes (if closed), take a few deep breaths, and notice their surroundings. The goal is to anchor them back into the reality of the room, away from the intense focus on past memories.

2. Review of the Session: A brief discussion about the session's experience allows the individual to verbalize their feelings and thoughts post-processing. It's an opportunity for the therapist to assess the client's emotional state and provide reassurance.

3. Grounding Techniques: To further ensure that the individual feels stable before leaving, grounding techniques are employed. These can include exercises such as feeling one's feet on the ground, holding a comforting object, or visualizing a safe place. Such techniques help dissipate any residual emotional or physical tension.

4. Positive Affirmations: The therapist may remind the individual of the positive beliefs or affirmations that were installed during the session. This reinforcement helps solidify the gains made during therapy and boosts the individual's confidence in their ability to cope with distressing memories.

5. Debriefing on Self-Care: Before concluding, the therapist provides guidance on self-care strategies that the individual can use between sessions. This might include activities that promote relaxation, journaling to process thoughts and feelings, or engaging in physical exercise to release tension.

6. Safety Plan: For individuals who might still feel vulnerable, creating a brief safety plan for the period immediately following the session is essential. This plan could outline steps to take if they experience heightened emotions or distress and include contact information for support.

7. Scheduling the Next Session: Setting up the next appointment gives the individual a clear sense of continuity in their therapy process. It reinforces the ongoing support they have and provides a future point of focus for further healing.

8. Encouragement and Support: The therapist concludes the session by offering words of encouragement, emphasizing the individual's strength and progress. This support is vital for building the person's confidence in their healing journey.

The Closure phase is not merely a procedural end to the session but a critical component of the EMDR therapy process. It ensures that individuals leave feeling empowered, with a sense of closure from the session's work, and equipped with tools to maintain their emotional equilibrium. This phase underscores the therapy's holistic approach, acknowledging the importance of emotional safety and stability in the healing process.

6.8: Reevaluation: Monitoring Progress Over Time

Reevaluation is a critical phase in the EMDR therapy process, serving as a cornerstone for both the therapist and the individual undergoing treatment. This phase is dedicated to assessing the progress made and determining the next steps in the therapeutic journey. It is during this stage that the effectiveness of the treatment is carefully evaluated, ensuring that the goals set at the outset are being met or adjusted according to the individual's evolving needs. The importance of this phase cannot be overstated, as it provides a structured opportunity to reflect on the changes that have occurred, celebrate successes, and identify areas that may require further attention.

The process of reevaluation involves a thorough review of the individual's current state in comparison to their condition at the beginning of therapy. This comparison is not limited to a mere recounting of symptoms but encompasses a deep dive into the individual's emotional well-being, behavioral changes, and improvements in relationships and daily functioning. The therapist and individual collaboratively explore the impact of therapy on various aspects of the individual's life, including stress levels, anxiety, coping mechanisms, and overall quality of life. This comprehensive assessment allows for a nuanced understanding of the individual's journey through EMDR therapy, highlighting both the strides made and the hurdles that remain.

Key components of the reevaluation phase include:

- **Assessment of Symptom Reduction**: A detailed discussion about any decrease in symptoms of trauma, anxiety, depression, or other mental health issues the individual was facing. This often involves revisiting the scales or questionnaires used at the beginning of therapy to quantify changes.

- **Evaluation of Behavioral Changes**: An analysis of any new behaviors or coping strategies the individual has adopted. This might include how they handle stress, interact in relationships, or confront challenging situations differently than before.

- **Feedback on the Therapy Process**: The individual's perspective on the therapy process is invaluable. Their feedback on what has been most helpful or challenging can guide future sessions and adjustments to the treatment plan.

- **Identification of Remaining Challenges**: Recognizing that healing is a journey, this step involves acknowledging any ongoing issues or new challenges that have emerged. It is an honest appraisal of work that still needs to be done.

- **Setting New Goals**: Based on the progress made and the challenges that remain, new therapeutic goals may be set. This could involve deepening the work on certain issues, addressing new areas of concern, or focusing on maintaining gains and preventing relapse.

- **Planning for Future Sessions**: With new or adjusted goals in mind, the therapist and individual plan the next steps. This might involve scheduling more sessions, trying different EMDR protocols, or incorporating complementary therapies.

The reevaluation phase is not a one-time event but a recurring element of EMDR therapy, ensuring that the therapy remains dynamic and responsive to the individual's needs. It reinforces the collaborative nature of the therapeutic relationship, empowering individuals to take an active role in their healing process. Through this ongoing assessment, individuals gain insight into their growth, learn to navigate setbacks with resilience, and continue to build upon their successes. This phase underscores the notion that healing is not linear but a continuous journey of self-discovery and transformation.

Chapter 7. How Bilateral Stimulation Works

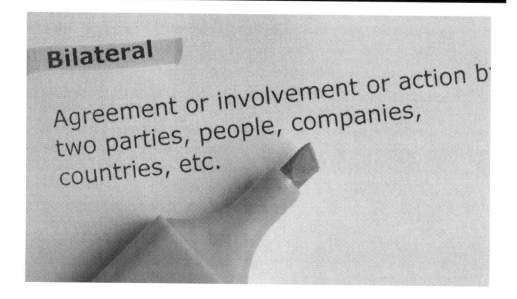

Bilateral

Agreement or involvement or action by two parties, people, companies, countries, etc.

7.1: Eye Movements, Tapping, and Auditory Stimulation

Eye movements in EMDR therapy are designed to mimic the natural process that occurs during Rapid Eye Movement (REM) sleep, a phase associated with the processing of day-to-day emotional experiences. By intentionally directing the eyes to move back and forth, the therapy facilitates the neurological process of connecting and processing stored memories, emotions, and thoughts that are causing distress. This bilateral stimulation encourages the brain to reprocess these memories, reducing their emotional impact and allowing the individual to develop new, healthier associations.

Tapping, another form of bilateral stimulation used in EMDR, involves alternating taps on different sides of the body. This method can be particularly effective for individuals who may find the eye movement component challenging or for those who respond more strongly to tactile stimuli. Tapping provides a rhythmic pattern that helps to focus the mind and body, creating a soothing effect that can reduce anxiety and stress levels. It supports the brain's natural ability to process and integrate traumatic memories by engaging both hemispheres, promoting emotional healing and cognitive restructuring.

Auditory stimulation, which includes sounds that alternate between the left and right ear, leverages the auditory system's capacity to process bilateral stimuli, further supporting the brain's natural healing processes. This form of stimulation can be particularly beneficial for individuals who are auditory learners or who have visual impairments that make eye movement difficult. The auditory cues help to engage the brain's attention and facilitate the processing of traumatic memories, leading to a decrease in emotional distress associated with those memories.

The effectiveness of these techniques lies in their ability to engage the brain's natural adaptive information processing mechanisms. By activating these mechanisms through bilateral stimulation, EMDR therapy helps individuals reprocess traumatic memories in a way that reduces their lingering effects, leading to improved emotional well-being. Each of these methods—eye movements, tapping, and auditory stimulation—offers a unique pathway to healing, allowing therapists to tailor the treatment to the individual needs of each person. The choice of technique can depend on the individual's preferences, the nature of their trauma, and their response to initial treatment sessions. The goal is always the same: to facilitate the processing of traumatic memories, reduce their emotional impact, and support the individual in developing healthier coping mechanisms and beliefs.

7.2: How Bilateral Stimulation Balances the Brain

The concept of **bilateral stimulation** is central to understanding how Eye Movement Desensitization and Reprocessing (EMDR) therapy facilitates emotional healing and cognitive integration. This process is rooted in the brain's inherent capacity for adaptive information processing, which can become blocked or imbalanced due to traumatic experiences or intense stress. Bilateral stimulation, whether through eye movements, auditory signals, or tactile feedback, acts as a catalyst for re-establishing the natural flow of communication between the brain's two hemispheres. This interhemispheric communication is crucial for processing and integrating traumatic memories, as it allows for the synthesis of emotional and cognitive experiences into a cohesive whole.

The left and right hemispheres of the brain have distinct yet complementary functions. The left hemisphere is generally associated with logical thinking, language, and analytical processing, while the right hemisphere is more involved with creativity, intuition, and emotional processing. When a person experiences trauma or severe stress, the ability to process and integrate these experiences can become compartmentalized, with the emotional intensity of the memory becoming isolated from the narrative or logical understanding of the event. This disconnection can lead to persistent symptoms such as flashbacks, anxiety, and emotional dysregulation, as the traumatic memory remains "stuck" without being fully processed.

Bilateral stimulation works by simultaneously engaging both hemispheres of the brain, promoting the integration of emotional and cognitive aspects of the memory. For example, as the individual recalls a distressing memory during an EMDR session, the bilateral stimulation may help link the intense emotions and physical sensations associated with the memory to the more analytical, narrative aspects processed by the left hemisphere. This integration helps to diminish the distressing power of the memory, allowing the individual to view their experience from a more balanced and less emotionally charged perspective.

Furthermore, this process can lead to a decrease in the physiological arousal associated with the traumatic memory, as the brain begins to recognize that the memory no longer poses an immediate threat. This reduction in arousal is a key component of the therapeutic effect of EMDR, as it allows the individual to approach their memories with increased calmness and clarity. Additionally, the rhythmic pattern of bilateral stimulation can have a soothing effect, similar to the relaxation experienced during certain types of meditation or deep breathing exercises. This calming effect can further facilitate the processing of traumatic memories by reducing the individual's level of stress and anxiety during therapy sessions.

The effectiveness of bilateral stimulation in balancing the brain and promoting emotional healing is supported by research indicating changes in brain activity following EMDR therapy. Neuroimaging studies have shown increased connectivity and activation in areas of the brain involved in memory processing and emotional regulation, suggesting that EMDR can help restore the brain's natural ability to heal from psychological trauma.

In practice, the application of bilateral stimulation requires careful consideration and customization to the needs of the individual. The therapist must assess the most effective form of stimulation for each person, whether it be eye movements, auditory tones, or tactile feedback, and adjust the pace and intensity of the stimulation to optimize the therapeutic effect. This personalized approach ensures that the individual feels safe and supported throughout the process, enhancing the efficacy of the therapy and the individual's overall experience of healing.

By fostering a deeper understanding of how bilateral stimulation contributes to the balancing of the brain and the integration of traumatic memories, individuals undergoing EMDR therapy can approach their healing journey with increased confidence and hope. The knowledge that there is a biologically grounded method for addressing the impacts of trauma can be empowering, offering a pathway to emotional freedom and resilience.

Chapter 8. Beyond Trauma: Everyday Applications of EMDR

8.1: Managing Everyday Stress and Anxiety

Incorporating Eye Movement Desensitization and Reprocessing (EMDR) into daily life offers a transformative approach for individuals grappling with stress and anxiety. This technique, originally designed for trauma recovery, has proven equally effective in managing the everyday pressures that can lead to overwhelming feelings of anxiety. The core of EMDR's application in daily stress management lies in its ability to reprocess and desensitize individuals to stressors, thereby reducing their impact and enhancing overall emotional well-being.

Grounding Techniques:

A foundational step in using EMDR for stress and anxiety involves grounding techniques. These practices help individuals anchor themselves in the present moment, creating a sense of stability that is crucial for managing acute stress. Techniques such as focused breathing, mindfulness meditation, and sensory awareness exercises serve as preparatory steps, enabling individuals to approach EMDR exercises from a place of calm.

Bilateral Stimulation:

At the heart of EMDR is bilateral stimulation, which can be adapted for self-help purposes to manage anxiety. Simple bilateral tapping, which involves alternately tapping the knees or hands, can be easily integrated into daily routines. This form of stimulation helps to activate both hemispheres of the brain, facilitating the processing of emotional distress and leading to a reduction in anxiety levels.

Visualization Techniques:

Visualization exercises, another key component of EMDR, allow individuals to confront stressors in a safe, controlled mental environment. By visualizing a place of safety or calm while engaging in bilateral stimulation, individuals can begin to reframe their relationship with stressors, reducing their emotional impact.

Positive Affirmations:

Incorporating positive affirmations during EMDR exercises can reinforce a sense of personal safety and resilience. Repeating affirmations such as "I am calm and in control" during bilateral stimulation can strengthen the individual's ability to manage stress and anxiety.

Journaling:

Coupling EMDR techniques with journaling offers a reflective practice for identifying and processing stressors. Writing about daily stressors and their emotional impact, followed by EMDR exercises, can aid in detaching from and reprocessing these stressors.

Safe Space Imagery:

Creating a mental image of a safe, peaceful place is a powerful EMDR technique for anxiety management. When faced with stress, mentally visiting this place while practicing bilateral stimulation can provide immediate relief and a sense of emotional safety.

Regular Practice:

Consistency is key in harnessing the benefits of EMDR for stress and anxiety management. Establishing a routine that includes EMDR exercises can enhance their effectiveness, making it easier to manage daily stressors.

Professional Guidance:

While many EMDR techniques can be practiced independently, consulting with a trained EMDR therapist is recommended for individuals facing severe anxiety or those interested in deeper exploration of this therapy. A professional can provide tailored guidance and support for integrating EMDR into one's daily life.

By adopting these EMDR techniques, individuals can equip themselves with practical tools for navigating the complexities of daily stress and anxiety. The adaptability of EMDR makes it a valuable resource for anyone seeking to improve their emotional resilience and achieve a greater sense of peace in their everyday lives.

8.2: Enhancing Relationships with EMDR

Eye Movement Desensitization and Reprocessing therapy, while initially conceptualized for trauma recovery, has profound implications for enhancing empathy, communication, and the development of meaningful relationships in both personal and professional spheres. The technique's core principle, facilitating the processing of emotional distress, can be directly applied to improve interpersonal interactions by fostering a deeper understanding of one's own emotional responses and those of others.

Empathy Development:

One of the most significant benefits of EMDR in the context of relationships is its capacity to enhance empathy. By processing one's own past experiences and emotional blocks, individuals can achieve a greater understanding and sensitivity towards the experiences of others. This heightened empathy not only improves personal relationships but also enhances professional interactions, making for a more harmonious work environment.

Communication Skills:

Effective communication is often hindered by unprocessed emotional baggage. EMDR therapy aids in identifying and resolving these emotional blocks, leading to clearer and more constructive communication. As individuals become more attuned to their emotional responses and learn to manage them effectively, they find it easier to express their needs, listen actively, and respond to others in a more understanding and supportive manner.

Building Meaningful Relationships:

The ability to form and maintain meaningful relationships is significantly influenced by one's emotional health and resilience. EMDR therapy's role in improving self-awareness and emotional regulation directly contributes to the development of deeper, more meaningful connections with others. By resolving past traumas and emotional disturbances, individuals can approach relationships from a place of strength and openness, laying the foundation for lasting bonds.

Professional Relationships:

In the professional realm, EMDR's impact on emotional intelligence can lead to better teamwork, leadership, and conflict resolution skills. A deeper understanding of one's emotional triggers and responses helps in navigating the complexities of workplace relationships, making for a more effective and cohesive working environment.

Conflict Resolution:

Conflicts, whether personal or professional, often escalate due to a lack of understanding and empathy. EMDR therapy equips individuals with the tools to approach conflicts from a place of calm and understanding, focusing on resolution rather than escalation. This approach not only resolves conflicts more effectively but also strengthens relationships by demonstrating a commitment to understanding and cooperation.

Self-Reflection and Growth:

The introspective nature of EMDR therapy encourages ongoing self-reflection and personal growth, qualities that are invaluable in any relationship. By continuously striving to understand and improve oneself, individuals can contribute positively to their relationships, promoting a cycle of mutual growth and enrichment.

Incorporating EMDR techniques into daily life can thus play a crucial role in improving not only one's mental health but also the quality of one's relationships. Whether it's by enhancing empathy, improving communication skills, or fostering a deeper understanding of oneself and others, the benefits of EMDR extend far beyond the realm of trauma recovery. By applying these principles, individuals can achieve a greater sense of connection and fulfillment in their personal and professional lives, making for richer, more meaningful interactions with those around them.

8.3: Building Emotional Resilience with EMDR

Building emotional resilience through the application of Eye Movement Desensitization and Reprocessing (EMDR) techniques is a powerful strategy for individuals seeking to navigate daily challenges with greater ease and stability. Emotional resilience, the ability to bounce back from stress, adversity, and life's inevitable challenges, is not an innate trait but a skill that can be developed and strengthened over time. EMDR, with its roots in addressing and reprocessing traumatic memories, offers unique tools that can be adapted to foster resilience in the face of everyday stressors and anxieties.

Developing a Personal Toolkit:

One of the first steps in building emotional resilience is to create a personal toolkit of strategies and techniques that can be drawn upon in times of need. This toolkit might include specific EMDR exercises such as **bilateral tapping** or **guided visualizations** that have been shown to help reduce the intensity of stress and anxiety when they arise. By having a set of go-to strategies, individuals can feel more empowered and prepared to handle difficult situations.

Regular Practice and Application:

Just as physical exercise strengthens the body, regular practice of EMDR techniques strengthens the mind's resilience to stress. Incorporating these practices into a daily or weekly routine can help to gradually build up one's emotional resilience. This could involve setting aside time each day for a short session of bilateral tapping or engaging in guided visualizations several times a week. Consistency is key to seeing long-term benefits.

Mindfulness and Emotional Awareness:

Mindfulness, a core component of emotional resilience, involves being present and fully engaged with the current moment without judgment. EMDR's focus on mindfulness and awareness can aid individuals in becoming more attuned to their emotional states and triggers. Through practices such as **mindful breathing** while focusing on a specific issue or stressor, individuals can learn to observe their emotions without being overwhelmed by them, allowing for a more measured and resilient response to challenges.

Positive Reframing and Cognitive Flexibility:

EMDR encourages the reprocessing of negative thoughts and beliefs that can undermine resilience. By identifying and challenging these negative patterns, individuals can learn to reframe their thoughts in a more positive and adaptive manner. This cognitive flexibility is a hallmark of emotional resilience, enabling individuals to view setbacks as opportunities for growth and learning rather than insurmountable obstacles.

Building a Support Network:

Emotional resilience is not just an individual endeavor; it can also be strengthened through connections with others. EMDR emphasizes the importance of a supportive network, whether through group therapy sessions or sharing experiences with friends and family. Knowing that one has a reliable support system can provide additional strength and resilience in difficult times.

Self-Care and Compassion:

Finally, building emotional resilience through EMDR involves a strong emphasis on self-care and self-compassion. Recognizing the importance of taking care of oneself, both physically and emotionally, is crucial. This might include engaging in activities that promote relaxation and well-being, such as exercise, reading, or spending time in nature, as well as practicing self-compassion and kindness towards oneself during challenging times.

By integrating these EMDR-inspired techniques and principles into one's life, individuals can enhance their capacity to withstand and adapt to life's challenges. Emotional resilience is not about avoiding stress or adversity but learning to navigate these experiences with grace, strength, and a sense of personal agency. Through dedicated practice and application of these strategies, individuals can achieve a greater sense of emotional freedom and resilience, ready to face whatever life may bring with confidence and composure.

Part 2: Practicing EMDR for Yourself

Chapter 9: Creating Your Safe Space

9.1: Understanding Safe Spaces in Therapy

Creating a **safe space** within the context of therapy, and particularly within the framework of Eye Movement Desensitization and Reprocessing (EMDR), is foundational to fostering an environment where healing and emotional processing can occur. This concept extends beyond the physical environment of a therapist's office, encompassing a psychological state that individuals can learn to access wherever they are. A safe space is characterized by a sense of security, acceptance, and freedom from judgment, allowing individuals to explore and express their emotions, thoughts, and memories without fear of criticism or harm.

The significance of establishing such a space lies in its role as a precondition for effective therapy. In the absence of safety, the mind's defenses remain up, hindering the processing of traumatic memories or stressful experiences. EMDR therapy, with its focus on accessing and reprocessing these memories, requires a baseline level of emotional safety to be effective. Without this, the bilateral stimulation techniques central to EMDR cannot achieve their full therapeutic potential.

Grounding techniques play a crucial role in creating and maintaining this sense of safety. These techniques, which can include focused breathing, mindfulness exercises, and sensory engagement, help individuals anchor themselves in the present moment, providing a counterbalance to the distress that may arise when confronting difficult memories. By establishing a practice of grounding before, during, and after EMDR sessions, individuals can enhance their ability to navigate emotional challenges with greater stability.

Visualization of a safe place is another powerful tool in the creation of a psychological safe space. This involves the detailed imagining of a place where one feels completely secure, calm, and content. The visualization should engage all the senses, making the imagined place as vivid and comforting as possible. During EMDR sessions, recalling this safe place can serve as a mental retreat, offering solace and respite when the therapeutic work becomes emotionally taxing.

Positive affirmations are also integral to reinforcing the safety of this space. Affirmations such as "I am safe," "I am in control," and "I can handle my emotions" can help build an internal dialogue that supports resilience and self-compassion. These affirmations, especially when combined with bilateral stimulation or grounding techniques, can strengthen the individual's sense of security and self-efficacy.

The creation of a personal sanctuary, whether through physical means in one's environment or through mental practices such as visualization and affirmations, is a dynamic process. It evolves as the individual's needs and therapeutic journey change. What remains constant is the core purpose of the safe space: to provide a secure foundation from which individuals can explore their emotions, confront their traumas, and embark on a path toward healing and emotional freedom.

The ability to cultivate such a space, both within the therapeutic setting and independently, empowers individuals to take an active role in their healing process. It underscores the principle that safety, both physical and emotional, is not just a basic need but a vital therapeutic tool. By learning to create and access their safe space, individuals can enhance the effectiveness of EMDR therapy, supporting their journey toward emotional well-being and resilience.

9.2: Grounding Techniques to Reduce Stress

Sensory Anchoring is another pivotal technique to establish a sense of present-moment awareness and reduce stress. This method involves focusing on one or more of your five senses to ground yourself in the here and now. For instance, holding a small, smooth stone in your hand and focusing on its texture, temperature, and weight can serve as a powerful anchor to the present, diverting your mind from stressors and anxieties.

Deep Breathing exercises are fundamental grounding techniques that can be performed anywhere, anytime. A simple yet effective practice is the 4-7-8 technique, where you breathe in through your nose for 4 seconds, hold your breath for 7 seconds, and exhale slowly through your mouth for 8 seconds. This exercise helps regulate the body's response to stress by activating the parasympathetic nervous system, promoting a state of calm.

Mindful Walking combines physical activity with mindfulness, creating a dynamic grounding experience. Choose a quiet place to walk, and as you move, pay close attention to the sensation of your feet touching the ground, the rhythm of your steps, and the feeling of the air on your skin. This practice not only helps in reducing stress but also enhances your physical well-being.

Nature Engagement offers a rich source of sensory experiences for grounding. Spending time in nature, whether it's a park, a garden, or near a body of water, can have a soothing effect on the mind and body. Focus on the sounds of birds, the sight of greenery, the smell of flowers, or the feel of the breeze. These natural elements can help shift your focus away from stress and towards a peaceful state of mind.

Progressive Muscle Relaxation (PMR) is a technique that involves tensing and then relaxing different muscle groups in the body. This practice can help identify areas of tension and promote relaxation. Starting from the toes and moving upwards through the legs, torso, arms, and face, tense each muscle group for a few seconds, then release. This method is particularly effective in reducing physical symptoms of stress and can enhance your sense of bodily awareness and relaxation.

Incorporating these grounding techniques into your daily routine can significantly impact your ability to manage stress and anxiety. Regular practice can help you develop a deeper connection to the present moment, enabling you to navigate life's challenges with greater ease and stability. Remember, the key to benefiting from these practices is consistency and mindfulness, allowing you to cultivate a sense of calm and resilience over time.

9.3: Guided Exercises for a Protective Mental Space

Exercise 1: Visualization of a Safe Place

Objective: The goal of this exercise is to help you create a mental image of a place where you feel completely safe, calm, and comfortable. This visualization can serve as a refuge during moments of stress or anxiety, providing a mental escape to a serene environment where you can regain a sense of peace and safety.

Step-by-step instructions:

1. Find a Quiet Space: Choose a quiet and comfortable place where you can sit or lie down without being disturbed. Ensure the environment is conducive to relaxation, perhaps dimming the lights or sitting in a comfortable chair or on a cushion.

2. Relax Your Body: Close your eyes and take a few deep breaths. Inhale slowly through your nose, hold for a moment, and then exhale slowly through your mouth. Repeat this process several times until you feel your body start to relax.

3. Imagine Your Safe Place: Begin to form a mental image of a place where you feel completely safe and at ease. This could be a real place you've visited before, a space you've created in your imagination, or a combination of both. Focus on the details—what does this place look like? What colors do you see? Are there any sounds? What is the temperature like?

4. Engage Your Senses: Deepen the visualization by engaging all your senses. Imagine the sounds you might hear in this place, the scents you might smell, and the textures you might feel. Perhaps there's a gentle breeze on your skin or the soft murmur of water nearby. The more vividly you can engage your senses, the more real the place will feel.

5. Anchor Yourself in the Space: Once your safe place is clearly visualized, find a spot within it where you can sit or stand. Imagine yourself being there, feeling completely protected and at ease. Notice the sense of safety and calm enveloping you.

6. Use a Cue to Reinforce the Visualization: Choose a word, phrase, or gesture to serve as a cue to bring you back to this place whenever you need it. It could be something like "peace," a gentle tapping of your finger, or a visual symbol that represents safety to you.

7. Gradually Return: When you're ready, slowly bring your awareness back to the present. Wiggle your fingers and toes, take a deep breath, and open your eyes. Remind yourself that you can return to this safe place in your mind whenever you wish.

8. Practice Regularly: The more you practice this visualization, the easier it will be to access your safe place during times of need. Try to perform this exercise daily or whenever you feel the need to find peace and safety.

Common pitfalls:

- **Rushing the Process:** It's important not to rush through the steps. Each phase of relaxation and visualization is crucial for creating a vivid and comforting safe place.

- **Getting Discouraged:** If you find it difficult to visualize at first, don't get discouraged. Visualization is a skill that improves with practice.

- **Distractions:** External noises or interruptions can disrupt the process. Try to ensure you won't be disturbed before starting the exercise.

Progress tracking:

Keep a journal of your experiences with this exercise. Note any changes in your ability to visualize your safe place and any differences in your feelings of stress or anxiety before and after the exercise. Over time, you may find it easier to enter your safe place and feel its calming effects more strongly.

Exercise 2: Breathing Techniques for Relaxation

Objective: Learn and practice breathing techniques to promote relaxation, reduce stress, and create a protective mental environment. This exercise aims to help you develop a quick and effective method to calm your mind and body, fostering a sense of safety and tranquility that supports emotional well-being.

Step-by-step instructions:

1. Find a Comfortable Position: Sit or lie down in a quiet, comfortable space where you won't be disturbed. Ensure your back is supported, and you can relax fully.

2. Close Your Eyes: Gently close your eyes. This helps to reduce visual distractions and focus inwardly.

3. Focus on Your Breath: Pay attention to your natural breathing pattern without trying to change it. Notice the air entering and leaving your nostrils or mouth and the rise and fall of your chest or abdomen.

4. Deepen Your Breath: Slowly inhale through your nose, counting to four. Feel your abdomen expand with air like a balloon. Hold your breath for a count of four.

5. Exhale Slowly: Exhale through your mouth for a count of six, consciously releasing tension and stress as the air leaves your body. Imagine expelling negative thoughts and emotions with each breath out.

6. Repeat the Cycle: Continue this breathing pattern for several minutes—inhale for four, hold for four, exhale for six. With each cycle, allow yourself to sink deeper into relaxation.

7. Return to Normal Breathing: After practicing this technique for 5-10 minutes, let your breathing return to its natural rhythm. Notice any changes in your body or mind.

8. Gently Open Your Eyes: When you feel ready, slowly open your eyes. Take a moment to observe how you feel before getting up.

Common pitfalls:

- **Forgetting to breathe through the diaphragm:** Many people breathe shallowly, using their chest. Ensure you're breathing deeply into your abdomen for maximum relaxation.

- **Rushing the process:** It's important not to rush through the steps. Each phase of the breath cycle should be slow and deliberate to promote relaxation.

- **Becoming frustrated if distracted:** It's normal for your mind to wander. Gently acknowledge any thoughts and return your focus to your breath without judgment.

Progress tracking:

Note your stress level on a scale of 1-10 before and after the exercise. Observing a decrease in stress levels can be motivating and affirm the benefits of the practice.

Keep a journal of your practice. Documenting your experience, including how long you practiced and any changes in your emotional or physical state, can help you establish a consistent routine and identify patterns over time.

Exercise 3: Positive Affirmations for Safety

Objective: To cultivate a sense of safety and emotional security through the practice of positive affirmations, reinforcing your mental safe space.

Step-by-step instructions:

1. Select Your Affirmations: Begin by choosing 3 to 5 affirmations that resonate with you and affirm safety, security, and well-being. Examples include "I am safe and secure," "I am surrounded by peace and protection," and "With every breath, I release anxiety and embrace calm."

2. Create a Comfortable Environment: Find a quiet, comfortable space where you won't be disturbed. You may choose to sit or lie down, whichever feels most comfortable for your body.

3. Practice Mindful Breathing: Before starting with your affirmations, take a few deep, slow breaths. Inhale through your nose, allowing your abdomen to expand, and exhale through your mouth, releasing any tension.

4. Repeat Your Affirmations: Close your eyes and silently repeat your chosen affirmations to yourself. With each repetition, visualize the words wrapping around you like a protective blanket, reinforcing your sense of safety and peace.

5. Visualize a Safe Space: As you continue to repeat your affirmations, imagine yourself in a place where you feel completely safe and at ease. This could be a real place or a space you create in your mind. Focus on the details of this place—the sights, sounds, and how secure it makes you feel.

6. Incorporate Sensory Details: Enhance the visualization by incorporating sensory details. Imagine the warmth of sunlight on your skin, the gentle sound of waves, or the scent of fresh earth after rain—whatever makes your safe space more vivid and comforting.

7. Anchor the Feeling: Once you feel deeply connected to your sense of safety, choose a physical gesture as an anchor (e.g., placing a hand over your heart or clasping your hands together). This physical touch will serve as a reminder of the safety and calm you can access anytime.

8. Gradually Return: After spending a few minutes in your safe space, gently bring your awareness back to the present. Wiggle your fingers and toes, take a deep breath, and open your eyes when ready.

9. Practice Regularly: Commit to practicing these affirmations daily, especially during moments of stress or anxiety, to reinforce your mental safe space and cultivate a lasting sense of security.

Common pitfalls:

- **Skipping Visualization:** Merely repeating affirmations without engaging in visualization can reduce their effectiveness. The mental imagery is crucial for emotional and psychological impact.

- **Inconsistency:** Sporadic practice limits the benefits. Regular repetition enhances the affirmations' power to transform thought patterns.

Progress tracking:

Journaling: Keep a journal to note any changes in your feelings of safety and anxiety levels. Record the affirmations that resonate most and any new ones you create.

Reflect on Changes: Periodically reflect on any shifts in your response to stress or anxiety. Note moments when you felt a strong sense of safety and what may have contributed to it.

Exercise 4: Grounding Techniques for Stability

Objective: To learn and apply grounding techniques that foster emotional and physical stability during moments of stress or disconnection.

Step-by-step instructions:

1. Find a Quiet Space: Begin by finding a quiet and comfortable space where you won't be disturbed. This can be anywhere that feels safe and calming to you.

2. Focus on Your Breath: Sit or stand comfortably. Close your eyes if it feels right for you, and turn your attention to your breathing. Take deep, slow breaths, inhaling through your nose and exhaling through your mouth. Aim for each inhale and exhale to last about 5 seconds.

3. Engage Your Senses: Slowly open your eyes and name out loud:

  - 5 things you can see,

  - 4 things you can touch,

  - 3 things you can hear,

  - 2 things you can smell, and

  - 1 thing you can taste.

4. Physical Grounding: Press your feet firmly into the ground. Imagine roots growing from the soles of your feet, deep into the earth. Visualize these roots anchoring you, providing stability and strength.

5. Use a Grounding Object: Hold a small object (a stone, a small toy, a piece of jewelry) in your hand. Focus on its texture, temperature, and weight. Let it serve as a physical anchor, bringing your mind to the present moment.

6. Mindful Observation: Choose an object in your immediate environment and focus all your attention on it. Notice every detail about its shape, color, texture, and any movements it might have. Spend a few minutes in this observation to anchor your mind in the now.

7. Stretch and Move: Gently stretch your body or stand up and move around if you've been sitting. Pay attention to the movement of each part of your body and how it feels as you stretch or move.

8. Reflect and Journal: After completing these steps, take a moment to reflect on the experience. If possible, jot down any thoughts, feelings, or sensations you observed during the exercise in a journal.

Common pitfalls:

- **Skipping Steps:** Each step is designed to gradually bring you into a state of groundedness. Avoid the temptation to skip steps, especially when time is short.

- **Rushing Through the Exercise:** The effectiveness of grounding techniques lies in their ability to slow down your mind and body. Rushing through the steps can reduce their impact.

- **Overanalyzing:** Try not to overthink the sensations or experiences. Allow yourself to simply observe and acknowledge them without judgment.

Progress tracking:

Frequency of Practice: Note how often you practice these grounding techniques and any variations in your experience over time.

Emotional and Physical Notes: Keep track of any changes in your emotional or physical state before and after the exercise. This can help you identify the techniques that are most effective for you.

Journaling: Regularly update your journal with reflections on your grounding practice. Include any new insights or adjustments you've made to the exercise to better suit your needs.

Exercise 5: Creating a Personal Sanctuary

Objective: To create a personal sanctuary in your mind, a safe and peaceful space that you can visit anytime you need to reduce stress, manage anxiety, or simply seek a moment of peace. This mental space will serve as a protective environment where you can feel secure, calm, and centered, no matter what's happening in your external world.

Step-by-step instructions:

1. Find a Quiet Space: Begin by finding a quiet and comfortable place where you can sit or lie down without interruptions. Ensure your environment is conducive to relaxation and free from distractions.

2. Close Your Eyes and Breathe: Close your eyes gently and focus on your breathing. Take deep, slow breaths to help you relax. With each exhale, imagine releasing any tension or stress from your body.

3. Visualize Your Sanctuary: In your mind's eye, start to construct your personal sanctuary. This can be any place that makes you feel safe and at peace. It could be a real place you've visited, a serene landscape, a cozy room, or even a fantastical setting. There are no limits to what this space can be.

4. Engage Your Senses: Enhance your sanctuary by engaging all your senses. Imagine what you see, hear, smell, touch, and even taste in this special place. The more vivid the details, the more real it will feel. For example, if you're in a forest, see the green of the trees, hear the birds singing, smell the earth after rain, feel the texture of the moss, and taste the fresh air.

5. Identify a Safe Spot: Within your sanctuary, identify a spot where you feel especially safe and comfortable. It could be a cozy corner, a soft patch of grass, or a warm, sunny spot. This is where you can return to in your visualization whenever you need solace.

6. Invite Positive Energy: Imagine a warm, glowing light in your sanctuary that represents positive energy. See this light enveloping you, filling you with a sense of peace, safety, and well-being.

7. Use an Anchor: Create an anchor to help you return to this space easily. It could be a word, a phrase, or a simple gesture. This anchor will serve as a shortcut to your sanctuary whenever you need it.

8. Gradually Return: When you're ready, slowly bring your awareness back to the present. Gently wiggle your fingers and toes, and when you feel ready, open your eyes.

9. Reflect: Take a moment to reflect on your experience. Consider keeping a journal to note what your sanctuary looks like and how it evolves over time.

Common pitfalls:

- **Getting Discouraged:** If you find it difficult to visualize at first, don't be discouraged. Visualization is a skill that improves with practice.

- **Distractions:** External noises or internal thoughts may distract you. Acknowledge them without judgment and gently redirect your focus back to your sanctuary.

Progress tracking:

Journaling: Keep a record of your experiences in your sanctuary, noting any changes or additions you make to the space. Also, note how you feel before and after visiting your sanctuary.

Frequency of Visits: Track how often you visit your sanctuary and its impact on your stress and anxiety levels over time.

Chapter 10. Self-Help Techniques Inspired by EMDR

10.1: Bilateral Tapping Techniques

Bilateral tapping, a cornerstone technique inspired by EMDR, serves as a self-help tool to manage stress, anxiety, and emotional blocks. This method leverages the brain's innate ability to process information by simulating the rhythmic patterns found in REM sleep. Here, we delve into the specifics of performing bilateral tapping, ensuring clarity and accessibility for those new to this practice.

Step 1: Find a Comfortable and Quiet Space

Select an environment where you feel safe and can relax without interruptions. Comfort is key to facilitating focus and emotional processing.

Step 2: Identify Your Focus of Concern

Before beginning, pinpoint the specific issue or emotion you wish to address. It could be a feeling of anxiety, a recurring negative thought, or a stressful event. Hold this focus gently in your mind without delving deeply into associated emotions.

Step 3: Establish a Self-Rating Scale

Rate your distress level on a scale from 0 to 10, where 0 means no distress and 10 signifies extreme distress. This self-assessment helps in tracking your progress through the tapping process.

Step 4: Begin Bilateral Tapping

Using both hands, gently tap on your knees or thighs in an alternating pattern. Ensure the rhythm is steady and comfortable for you. If tapping feels uncomfortable, you can also alternate pressing your feet on the ground. The key is to maintain a rhythmic, bilateral pattern.

Step 5: Maintain Focus on the Issue

While tapping, keep your mind on the chosen issue or emotion. If your thoughts wander, gently bring them back to the focus of your concern.

Step 6: Observe Your Experience

Pay attention to any changes in your thoughts, emotions, or physical sensations. There's no right or wrong way to feel; simply notice what happens.

Step 7: Conclude and Reassess

After a few minutes, stop tapping and take a moment to relax. Reassess your distress level using the same 0 to 10 scale. Many find that their distress level decreases after tapping, though results can vary.

Step 8: Repeat if Necessary

If your distress level has not significantly decreased, you may repeat the process, perhaps focusing on different aspects of the issue or any new emotions that have surfaced.

Tips for Effective Bilateral Tapping:

- Ensure you are in a safe and comfortable environment where you won't be disturbed.
- Start with shorter sessions to accustom yourself to the process.
- Practice regularly, especially during times of lower stress, to build familiarity and effectiveness.

- If memories or emotions become too intense, take a break and consider seeking support from a trained professional.

Bilateral tapping can be a powerful technique for individuals looking to manage everyday stressors, emotional blocks, and anxiety. By integrating this practice into your self-care routine, you can harness your body's natural processing capabilities to foster emotional healing and resilience.

10.2: Guided Visualizations for Anxiety and Emotional Blocks

Guided visualizations are a transformative technique that leverages the power of the mind's eye to foster healing and emotional balance. This method involves directing the imagination to visualize a scenario that promotes peace, safety, and well-being. By engaging in this practice, individuals can create a mental refuge from stress and anxiety, facilitating a state of relaxation that permeates both mind and body. For those new to this practice, the following detailed steps offer a pathway to addressing anxiety and emotional blocks through guided visualization.

Step 1: Choose a Quiet and Comfortable Space

Select a location where you are unlikely to be interrupted. Comfort is crucial, as a relaxed body supports a focused and receptive state of mind. Ensure the environment is conducive to relaxation, perhaps dimming the lights or sitting in a comfortable chair.

Step 2: Use Deep Breathing to Center Yourself

Begin with several deep breaths, inhaling slowly through the nose and exhaling through the mouth. With each breath, imagine tension leaving your body, creating space for calm and peace to enter. This step is vital for preparing both body and mind for the visualization process.

Step 3: Engage Your Imagination

Close your eyes and picture a place where you feel completely at ease. This could be a real location or a landscape born from your creativity. Visualize this place in vivid detail—the colors, sounds, smells, and textures. Imagine yourself within this scene, fully immersed in its tranquility.

Step 4: Incorporate Bilateral Stimulation

While immersed in your visualization, introduce a form of bilateral stimulation such as tapping your thighs alternately or swaying gently from side to side. This action can enhance the effectiveness of the visualization, mimicking the therapeutic elements of EMDR by engaging both hemispheres of the brain.

Step 5: Introduce a Positive Affirmation

Within the safety of your imagined place, introduce a positive affirmation that resonates with your desired state of being. Phrases like "I am safe," "I am at peace," or "I am in control of my emotions" can be powerful. Repeat this affirmation gently, allowing its meaning to infuse your visualization with positivity and strength.

Step 6: Focus on Physical Sensations

Pay attention to any physical sensations that arise during your visualization. If you encounter areas of tension in your body, imagine directing breath and healing energy to these spots, visualizing the tension dissolving and being replaced by a sense of well-being.

Step 7: Gradually Return to the Present

After spending a few moments in your visualization, gently bring your awareness back to the present. Wiggle your fingers and toes, take a few deep breaths, and when you're ready, open your eyes. Carry the sense of calm and safety from your visualization into the rest of your day.

Step 8: Reflect on the Experience

Take a moment to reflect on the visualization process. Consider how it made you feel and whether it shifted your emotional state. Journaling about your experience can deepen the practice, providing insights into your emotional landscape and how visualization techniques can serve as a tool for managing anxiety and emotional blocks.

Incorporating guided visualization into your self-care routine can be a powerful way to harness the mind's ability to influence emotional and physical well-being. Regular practice strengthens the mind's capacity to retreat to a place of safety and calm, offering a respite from the stresses of daily life and a means to overcome deep-seated emotional blocks.

10.3: Safe Eye Movements for Self-Help

Eye movements, integral to Eye Movement Desensitization and Reprocessing (EMDR), offer a unique self-help approach for managing mild stress and enhancing self-awareness. This technique, inspired by the natural process of Rapid Eye Movement (REM) sleep, facilitates the brain's processing of emotional experiences. To engage in this practice safely and effectively, follow these detailed steps, ensuring a supportive environment for emotional processing.

Step 1: Secure a Peaceful Environment

Choose a location where you feel comfortable and free from interruptions. A calm setting is crucial for focusing inward and facilitating the eye movement process.

Step 2: Select a Mild Stressor

Think of a situation or thought that causes you mild stress, avoiding deeply traumatic memories for self-practice. Hold this stressor in mind lightly, without immersing yourself in associated emotions.

Step 3: Engage in Eye Movements

Begin by finding a point that you can comfortably focus on directly in front of you. Slowly move your eyes from side to side, following a horizontal path. It's essential to keep your head still, moving only your eyes. The pace should be steady and not too fast; a rhythm similar to that of a pendulum swinging is optimal.

Step 4: Maintain Focus on the Stressor

As you move your eyes back and forth, keep your mental focus on the mild stressor. Notice any thoughts, feelings, or sensations that arise, observing them without judgment.

Step 5: Grounding and Centering

After several sequences of eye movements, typically lasting a few minutes, pause to take a deep breath. Bring your focus back to the present moment, noticing the environment around you and any sensations in your body.

Step 6: Reflect on the Experience

Consider any changes in your perception of the mild stressor. Often, individuals report a decrease in emotional intensity related to the stressor. Reflecting on this shift can enhance self-awareness and understanding of personal stress patterns.

Step 7: Practice Regularly

Incorporate this technique into your routine, especially during times of mild stress. Regular practice can improve your ability to manage stress and increase emotional resilience.

Safety Considerations:

- If at any point you feel overwhelmed or experience an increase in distress, stop the exercise and ground yourself in the present by focusing on your breath or surroundings.

- This technique is intended for mild stressors. If dealing with more severe emotional issues, professional guidance from a trained EMDR therapist is recommended.

- Ensure that your practice environment is safe and that you are in a stable emotional state before beginning.

Enhancing the Practice:

- Combining eye movements with other self-help techniques, such as deep breathing or positive affirmations, can amplify the benefits.

- Journaling about your experience after each session can provide insights into your emotional patterns and progress over time.

Eye movement exercises, when performed with care and attention, can be a valuable tool for self-help, offering a pathway to greater emotional freedom and self-awareness. By engaging in this practice, you can harness your body's natural processing capabilities, facilitating personal growth and emotional well-being.

Chapter 11: Overcoming Emotional Blocks and Abreaction

11.1: Strategies to Overcome Feeling Stuck

When you find yourself feeling stuck during the practice of EMDR, it's crucial to recognize this as a common part of the healing process. Feeling stuck can manifest as an inability to move past a certain point in your emotional processing or finding yourself repeatedly confronting the same distressing memories without a sense of progression. Here are practical strategies to navigate through this stagnation and facilitate continued growth and healing.

Revisit Your Safe Space:

If you're feeling overwhelmed or stuck, taking a moment to mentally return to your safe space can help recalibrate your emotional state. This technique, established in the earlier phases of EMDR therapy, serves as a grounding mechanism, allowing you to temporarily step away from distressing memories and regain a sense of safety and control.

Adjust the Focus of Your Session:

Sometimes, the feeling of being stuck can be attributed to focusing too narrowly on a specific aspect of a memory or emotion. Broadening or shifting your focus to include different aspects of your experience can provide new insights and pathways for processing. For example, if you've been concentrating on the visual elements of a memory, try to explore the associated sounds, smells, or physical sensations.

Incorporate Movement:

Physical movement can be a powerful catalyst for emotional processing. Engaging in simple, bilateral movements such as walking, swaying, or tapping your feet on the ground while thinking about the stuck point can help facilitate the brain's processing capabilities and potentially provide a new perspective on the issue at hand.

Utilize Journaling:

Writing about your experiences, particularly the points where you feel stuck, can offer a different mode of processing that complements the EMDR therapy. Journaling allows for reflection and can often reveal underlying patterns or beliefs that are contributing to the blockage. It can also be a way to express emotions that are difficult to articulate verbally.

Seek External Support:

Discussing your feelings of being stuck with your therapist can provide valuable insights and adjustments to your therapy plan. Your therapist might suggest alternative approaches within the EMDR framework, such as changing the target memory or incorporating different bilateral stimulation techniques. Additionally, they can help ensure that your practice remains within a safe and therapeutic range, especially when navigating intense emotions or memories.

Practice Patience and Self-Compassion:

It's important to remember that healing is not a linear process, and feeling stuck does not mean you have failed or that EMDR is not working. Emotional processing involves complex layers of memories and feelings, and sometimes the system needs time to integrate these experiences fully. Practicing patience and offering yourself compassion during these times can be as crucial to your healing journey as any specific technique.

Engage in Mindfulness and Meditation:

Mindfulness practices can enhance your awareness of the present moment and help reduce the intensity of distressing memories or feelings. Simple breathing exercises or guided meditations can serve as effective tools for managing anxiety and stress, providing a calm and centered state from which to approach your EMDR practice.

Explore Creative Expression:

Sometimes, traditional verbal and cognitive approaches may not fully capture the depth of what you're experiencing. Creative outlets such as drawing, painting, or music can offer an alternative means of expression and processing, potentially unlocking new avenues for movement through areas where you feel stuck.

By employing these strategies, you can navigate the moments of feeling stuck with greater ease and continue on your path toward healing and emotional freedom. Remember, each step, no matter how small, is a valuable part of your journey.

11.2: Strategies to Manage Intense Emotional Reactions

Exercise 1: Emotional Awareness Journaling

Objective: To enhance emotional awareness and manage intense emotional reactions through the practice of journaling, enabling a deeper understanding of personal triggers and emotional patterns.

Step-by-step instructions:

1. Select a Journal: Choose a notebook or digital journal that feels personal and comfortable for you. This will be your dedicated space for emotional awareness journaling.

2. Set a Regular Schedule: Dedicate a specific time each day for journaling. Consistency is key to gaining insight into your emotional patterns and reactions.

3. Identify Your Emotional State: Begin each journaling session by noting your current emotional state. Use descriptive words or phrases to capture how you feel at the moment.

4. Reflect on the Day's Events: Write about the events of your day, focusing on those that evoked a strong emotional response. Describe the situation, your reaction, and the emotions you experienced.

5. Explore the Why: Delve deeper into each emotional response by asking yourself why you felt that way. Try to identify any triggers or underlying beliefs that may have influenced your reaction.

6. Consider Alternative Responses: Reflect on how you might respond differently in the future. Imagine a scenario where you handle the situation in a way that aligns more closely with your desired emotional state.

7. Note Patterns and Triggers: Over time, review your journal entries to identify patterns in your emotional reactions and the triggers that cause them. This awareness can be a powerful tool in managing intense emotions.

8. Set Goals for Emotional Growth: Based on your observations, set personal goals for emotional regulation and resilience. Use your journal to track progress towards these goals.

Common pitfalls:

- **Skipping Reflection Time:** Rushing through the journaling process without taking the time to truly reflect on your emotions and reactions can limit the effectiveness of this exercise.

- **Ignoring Patterns:** Failing to recognize and address recurring emotional patterns and triggers can hinder emotional growth and self-awareness.

- **Being Overly Critical:** Judging yourself harshly for your emotions or reactions can stifle honest reflection and self-compassion, which are essential for emotional awareness.

Progress tracking:

Weekly Reviews: At the end of each week, review your journal entries to summarize key emotional experiences, triggers, and progress towards your emotional regulation goals.

Emotional Growth Milestones: Note any significant breakthroughs or achievements in understanding and managing your emotions. Celebrate these milestones to encourage continued progress.

Exercise 2: Identifying Triggers and Patterns

Objective: The objective of this exercise is to help you identify specific triggers and patterns that lead to intense emotional reactions. By recognizing these triggers, you can begin to understand and manage your emotional responses more effectively, reducing the intensity and frequency of overwhelming feelings.

Step-by-step instructions:

1. **Create a Trigger Journal:** Start by keeping a journal dedicated to noting when you experience intense emotional reactions. Include the date, time, and a brief description of the situation.

2. **Note the Immediate Cause:** For each entry, write down what you believe triggered the emotional reaction. Was it something someone said? A particular situation? A memory?

3. **Describe Your Emotional Response:** Detail the emotions you felt during the incident. Try to name the emotions as specifically as possible, such as anger, sadness, fear, or frustration.

4. **Identify Physical Sensations:** Record any physical sensations you experienced. This could include a racing heart, tightness in your chest, trembling, or feeling hot or cold.

5. **Reflect on Past Experiences:** After you have several entries, review your journal to identify any patterns. Do certain types of situations, comments, or people consistently trigger you?

6. **Seek Common Themes:** Look for common themes in your triggers. Are they related to feelings of rejection, loss, failure, or something else? Identifying themes can help you understand deeper issues that may need addressing.

7. Plan for Future Triggers: Based on your identified triggers and themes, brainstorm strategies for managing these situations in the future. This might include deep breathing, taking a time-out, or using positive affirmations.

8. Implement Coping Strategies: The next time you encounter a known trigger, apply your chosen coping strategy. Note the outcome in your journal, including what worked and what didn't.

9. Adjust as Needed: Over time, refine your strategies based on what you learn from each experience. This is a process of trial and error, so be patient with yourself.

Common pitfalls:

- **Overlooking Subtle Triggers:** Some triggers may not be immediately obvious. Pay attention to subtle cues that may be affecting your emotional state.

- **Neglecting to Record Immediately:** The sooner you record the experience after it happens, the more accurate your account will be. Delaying might lead to forgetting important details.

- **Being Too Hard on Yourself:** Recognize that identifying and managing triggers is a challenging process. Be compassionate with yourself as you learn and grow.

Progress tracking:

Monitor Frequency and Intensity: Keep track of how often you experience intense emotional reactions and their intensity. Over time, you should see a decrease in both as you become better at managing your triggers.

Reflect on Coping Success: Regularly review your journal entries to assess which coping strategies are most effective for you. Celebrate your successes and consider how you can apply successful strategies to other triggers.

Exercise 3: Emotional Regulation through Art

Objective: To utilize art as a medium for expressing and regulating intense emotions, providing a non-verbal outlet for feelings that may be difficult to articulate. This exercise aims to facilitate emotional processing, reduce stress, and enhance self-awareness through creative expression.

Step-by-step instructions:

1. Gather Your Materials: Choose any art supplies you feel drawn to, such as paper, canvas, paints, markers, crayons, or clay. There's no need for professional-grade materials; use whatever you have available that allows you to express yourself freely.

2. Create a Comfortable Space: Set up a dedicated area where you can work undisturbed. Ensure it's a place where you feel safe and comfortable, with enough room to explore your artistic process.

3. Set an Intention: Before beginning, take a moment to focus on your current emotional state. Identify any intense emotions you're experiencing, such as anger, sadness, or anxiety. Set an intention to explore these emotions through your art, without judgment or expectation.

4. Express Freely: Begin creating your art, focusing on the process rather than the outcome. Let your emotions guide your choices of colors, shapes, and textures. If you're unsure where to start, simply make a mark on the page and allow your intuition to lead the way.

5. Notice Your Body's Reactions: As you work, pay attention to any sensations in your body. Artistic expression can evoke strong physical responses. If you notice tension or discomfort, take a break to breathe deeply and center yourself before continuing.

6. Reflect on Your Art: Once you feel your piece is complete, step back and observe it without critique. Reflect on the emotions that arose during the process and any insights you've gained about your emotional state.

7. Write About Your Experience: In a journal, write about what you created and how the process felt. Describe any challenges you encountered and how you dealt with them. Reflect on what your art expresses about your emotions and any new understandings you've reached.

8. Practice Regularly: Emotional regulation through art is a skill that deepens with practice. Aim to incorporate this exercise into your routine, experimenting with different mediums and techniques as you grow more comfortable with the process.

Common pitfalls:

- **Focusing Too Much on Technique:** Remember, the goal is emotional expression, not creating a masterpiece. Don't let concerns about your artistic ability hinder your process.

- **Judging Your Work:** It's easy to fall into self-criticism, especially when working with intense emotions. Remind yourself that the value lies in the process and the emotional release it provides, not in the aesthetic quality of the final product.

Progress tracking:

Document Your Artwork: Keep a visual diary of your artwork, noting the dates and emotions explored in each piece. Over time, you may notice patterns or themes that can provide further insight into your emotional landscape.

Reflect on Your Growth: Periodically review your journal entries and artwork to reflect on your emotional growth and changes in how you express and manage your emotions through art.

Exercise 4: Developing Emotional Resilience

Objective: To develop emotional resilience by practicing strategies to manage intense emotional reactions, enabling you to face stress and anxiety with greater stability and adaptability.

Step-by-step instructions:

1. Identify Emotional Triggers: Begin by reflecting on recent situations that have triggered intense emotional reactions. Note these triggers in a journal, focusing on what emotions they evoked and the circumstances surrounding them.

2. Practice Mindful Observation: When you notice an intense emotion arising, pause and observe it without judgment. Acknowledge the emotion ("I am feeling anxious") and breathe deeply, focusing on the physical sensations in your body associated with this emotion.

3. Label Your Emotions: Assign a name to what you are feeling. Research shows that labeling emotions can help reduce their intensity and make them more manageable. Use simple terms like "anger," "fear," or "sadness."

4. Challenge Negative Thoughts: Identify the thoughts accompanying your intense emotions. Challenge these thoughts by asking yourself evidence-based questions, such as "What evidence do I have that this thought is true?" or "Is there another way to view this situation?"

5. Engage in a Grounding Technique: Choose a grounding technique to bring yourself back to the present moment. This could be the "5-4-3-2-1" technique, where you identify five things you can see, four you can touch, three you can hear, two you can smell, and one you can taste.

6. Implement a Positive Activity: Engage in an activity that brings you joy or relaxation. This could be reading, taking a walk, practicing yoga, or listening to music. The goal is to shift your focus from the intense emotion to something positive.

7. Seek Support When Needed: If an emotional reaction feels overwhelming, reach out to a trusted friend, family member, or professional for support. Sharing your feelings can provide relief and new perspectives.

Common pitfalls:

- **Ignoring or suppressing emotions:** Acknowledging and accepting your emotions is crucial for managing them effectively.

- **Over-identifying with emotions:** Remember, you are not your emotions. They are temporary and do not define you or your capabilities.

- **Ruminating on negative thoughts:** This can intensify emotions. Focus on challenging and replacing these thoughts with more balanced ones.

Progress tracking:

Journaling: Keep a daily or weekly journal of your emotional triggers, the strategies you used to manage them, and the outcomes. Note any patterns or improvements over time.

Emotional Scale: Before and after applying these strategies, rate the intensity of your emotions on a scale of 1-10. Tracking these ratings can help you see your progress in managing emotional reactions.

Exercise 5: Practicing Self-Compassion Techniques

Objective: To develop and strengthen self-compassion through specific techniques, helping to manage intense emotional reactions and foster a kinder, more understanding relationship with oneself.

Step-by-step instructions:

1. **Identify Your Critical Inner Voice:** Notice when you're being self-critical. Write down a few of the most frequent critical thoughts you have about yourself.

2. **Challenge the Critic:** For each critical thought, challenge its validity. Ask yourself, "Is this really true?" and "Would I say this to a friend?" This helps to put distance between you and the critical voice.

3. **Cultivate a Compassionate Voice:** Create a compassionate response to each of the critical thoughts. This response should be understanding, kind, and supportive, much like what you would offer a good friend in distress.

4. **Practice Mindful Acceptance:** When you notice feelings of inadequacy or failure, pause and acknowledge these feelings without judgment. Say to yourself, "This is a moment of suffering, suffering is part of life."

5. **Use Soothing Touch:** Place your hand over your heart or another comforting place on your body. The physical touch can be a powerful way to convey warmth and compassion to yourself.

6. **Visualize Compassion:** Imagine a figure that embodies compassion (it could be a spiritual figure, a loved one, or an idealized compassionate version of yourself). Visualize this figure sending you compassion, understanding, and love.

7. Write a Compassionate Letter to Yourself: Write a letter from the perspective of an unconditionally loving and compassionate friend. Address the challenges you're facing and offer kindness and understanding.

8. Practice Regularly: Like any skill, self-compassion takes practice. Dedicate time each day to go through these steps, especially during periods of stress or self-criticism.

Common pitfalls:

- **Forgetting to Practice:** It's easy to forget to practice self-compassion, especially during busy or stressful times. Setting reminders can help maintain consistency.

- **Self-Judgment:** You might find yourself judging your attempts at self-compassion ("I'm not doing this right," "This feels silly"). Recognize this as just another form of self-criticism and gently redirect your focus back to the exercise.

- **Expecting Immediate Results:** Developing self-compassion is a gradual process. Don't get discouraged if you don't feel a significant change right away. Consistent practice over time leads to growth.

Progress tracking:

Journaling: Keep a journal of your self-compassion practices. Note any changes in your self-talk, how you handle difficult emotions, and any shifts in your overall well-being.

Emotional Check-ins: Regularly check in with yourself to assess how you're feeling. Note any patterns or changes in your emotional responses, particularly in situations that would have previously triggered a harsh self-critical reaction.

Chapter 12. Managing Everyday Anxiety and Stress

12.1: Identifying Triggers and Hidden Causes

Understanding the intricate patterns of triggers and their hidden causes is pivotal in managing everyday anxiety and stress. Triggers, often misunderstood, are specific stimuli that provoke a psychological or emotional response, potentially leading to anxiety or stress. These can range from external events, such as a demanding work environment, to internal cues, like negative self-talk. Identifying these triggers is the first step toward mitigating their impact on your emotional well-being.

Recognizing Patterns of Triggers:

The initial phase involves keen observation of your reactions to various situations. Keeping a journal can be an invaluable tool in this process. Document instances when you feel anxious or stressed, noting the environment, people involved, and your thoughts at the time. Over time, patterns may emerge, offering clues to your triggers. For example, you might find that crowded spaces consistently provoke anxiety, or certain interactions at work lead to stress.

Analyzing Recurrent Themes:

Once you've identified patterns, the next step is to delve deeper into the recurrent themes. Ask yourself what these triggers have in common. Is it a fear of judgment, a sense of overwhelm, or perhaps a feeling of lack of control? Understanding the underlying themes can provide insights into the emotional roots of your stress and anxiety.

Discovering Hidden Causes:

Some triggers are not immediately apparent and may require further introspection to uncover. Hidden causes often stem from past experiences or deeply ingrained beliefs about oneself or the world. For instance, a fear of failure might be linked to early educational experiences where high achievement was heavily emphasized. Recognizing these connections can be challenging but is crucial for addressing the root causes of your stress and anxiety.

Strategies for Identifying Triggers:

1. **Mindfulness Practice**:
   Engaging in mindfulness can enhance your awareness of the present moment, making it easier to identify when and how triggers affect you. Techniques such as focused breathing or body scans can help you become more attuned to your emotional responses.

2. **Behavioral Experiments**:
   Experimenting with different responses to potential triggers can help identify what specifically provokes stress or anxiety. For example, if speaking in meetings is a trigger, try various preparation techniques to see which reduces your anxiety.

3. **Seek Feedback**:
   Sometimes, an outside perspective can help identify triggers you might not have noticed. Trusted friends, family members, or therapists can offer insights into patterns of behavior or reactions that are not apparent to you.

Addressing Triggers: Identifying your triggers is an important step, but addressing them is where the real change occurs. For external triggers, consider strategies to modify your environment or your interaction with it. For internal triggers, cognitive-behavioral techniques can be effective in challenging and changing negative thought patterns. Techniques such as reframing thoughts or exposure therapy, gradually facing the trigger in a controlled manner, can also be beneficial.

Remember, the goal is not to eliminate all triggers, as this is often not possible, but to reduce their power over your emotional state. With patience and practice, you can learn to navigate your triggers more effectively, leading to reduced anxiety and stress in your daily life.

12.2: Exercises to Manage Anxiety in Specific Situations

Exercise 1: Managing Work-Related Anxiety

Objective: To develop strategies for managing work-related anxiety, enabling you to remain calm and focused under pressure, improve productivity, and maintain a healthy work-life balance.

Step-by-step instructions:

1. **Identify Specific Triggers:** Begin by noting situations at work that trigger your anxiety. This could be meetings, deadlines, presentations, or interactions with certain colleagues. Understanding your triggers is the first step in managing your response to them.

2. **Create a Pre-Event Routine:** For events that trigger anxiety, such as presentations or meetings, develop a routine to perform beforehand. This could include deep breathing exercises, positive affirmations, or visualizing a successful outcome to help calm your nerves.

3. **Establish Boundaries:** Set clear boundaries around work hours to ensure work-related stress does not encroach on your personal time. This might mean turning off email notifications after a certain hour or having a specific workspace that you can step away from at the end of the day.

4. **Break Tasks into Manageable Steps:** Large projects can seem overwhelming and trigger anxiety. Break them down into smaller, more manageable tasks and focus on completing one at a time.

5. **Use Relaxation Techniques:** Incorporate relaxation techniques into your daily routine, such as deep breathing, meditation, or progressive muscle relaxation, especially during breaks. These practices can help reduce overall stress levels and make it easier to manage work-related anxiety.

6. **Seek Support:** Talk to a trusted colleague, supervisor, or a mental health professional about your anxiety. Sharing your concerns can lighten your emotional load and they may offer helpful advice or accommodations.

7. **Practice Mindfulness:** Engage in mindfulness exercises, such as mindful walking or eating during your lunch break. Mindfulness can help you stay present and reduce anxiety by preventing worry about future tasks or ruminating on past events.

8. **Celebrate Achievements:** Regularly acknowledge and celebrate your accomplishments, no matter how small. This can help shift your focus from anxiety about tasks to recognition of your capabilities and successes.

Common pitfalls:

- **Ignoring Physical Health:** Neglecting physical health, including lack of sleep, poor diet, and no exercise, can exacerbate anxiety. Ensure you're taking care of your body to help manage stress levels.

- **Procrastination:** Putting off tasks can increase anxiety as deadlines approach. Try to tackle tasks early and use time management strategies to avoid last-minute stress.

- **Overcommitting:** Taking on more work than you can handle can lead to burnout and increased anxiety. Learn to say no or delegate tasks when necessary to manage your workload effectively.

Progress tracking:

Journaling: Keep a daily or weekly journal of your anxiety levels and the situations that trigger them. Note which strategies you used and how effective they were in managing your anxiety.

Set Specific Goals: Set clear, achievable goals for managing work-related anxiety, such as practicing deep breathing exercises daily or completing a mindfulness course. Track your progress towards these goals to stay motivated.

Exercise 2: Navigating Anxiety in Relationships

Objective: To develop strategies for managing anxiety within the context of personal and professional relationships, fostering healthier interactions and communication.

Step-by-step instructions:

1. **Identify Relationship Triggers:** Reflect on recent interactions in your relationships that have triggered anxiety. Note specific situations, words, or actions that heightened your stress levels.

2. **Analyze Your Reaction:** For each identified trigger, examine your immediate emotional and physical reactions. Recognize patterns in your responses that may be contributing to relationship stress.

3. **Develop a Response Plan:** Create a plan for how you can respond differently in future interactions. This might include taking deep breaths to calm yourself, using affirmations to bolster your confidence, or excusing yourself from a situation temporarily to regain composure.

4. **Practice Active Listening:** In conversations, focus fully on the other person's words, tone, and body language. Remind yourself to listen rather than planning your response while they are speaking. This can reduce anxiety by keeping you engaged in the present moment.

5. **Communicate Openly:** When you're feeling less anxious, communicate your feelings and needs clearly and respectfully. Use "I" statements to express how certain interactions make you feel without placing blame.

6. **Set Boundaries:** Identify what you need in relationships to feel safe and reduce anxiety. Communicate these needs clearly to others, setting boundaries where necessary to protect your emotional well-being.

7. **Seek Support:** If certain relationships consistently trigger anxiety, consider seeking support from a therapist or counselor. They can provide strategies for managing anxiety and improving communication skills.

8. **Reflect and Adjust:** After implementing these strategies, reflect on any changes in your anxiety levels and relationship dynamics. Adjust your approach as needed based on what you learn.

Common pitfalls:

- **Avoiding Difficult Conversations:** While it might seem easier to avoid conversations that trigger anxiety, this can lead to unresolved issues and increased stress. Practice facing these situations with prepared strategies.

- **Overgeneralizing:** Avoid assuming that all interactions will lead to anxiety. Recognize that each situation is unique and approach it with an open mind.

- **Neglecting Self-Care:** Managing anxiety in relationships can be draining. Ensure you're also taking time for self-care and activities that reduce stress and recharge your emotional batteries.

Progress tracking:

Journaling: Keep a journal of interactions that trigger anxiety, noting the situation, your response, and the outcome. Over time, review your entries to assess progress and identify areas for improvement.

Anxiety Levels: Rate your anxiety levels before and after significant interactions on a scale of 1-10. Tracking these ratings can help you gauge the effectiveness of your strategies over time.

Exercise 3: Coping with Unexpected Daily Challenges

Objective: Develop strategies to effectively manage and reduce anxiety triggered by unexpected daily challenges, enhancing your ability to remain calm and respond adaptively in unforeseen situations.

Step-by-step instructions:

1. **Identify Common Unexpected Challenges:** Start by reflecting on recent situations that caught you off guard and triggered anxiety. List these incidents to recognize patterns or common themes.

2. **Prepare Mental Responses:** For each type of unexpected challenge identified, prepare a mental script or affirmation that promotes calmness and perspective. For example, if unexpected work tasks are a common trigger, your script might be, "I can handle this one step at a time."

3. **Practice Deep Breathing:** Incorporate deep breathing exercises as an immediate response to unexpected stress. Breathe in slowly for a count of four, hold for four, and exhale for eight. This helps activate your body's relaxation response.

4. **Visualize Positive Outcomes:** For each unexpected challenge, spend a few minutes visualizing a calm and successful response to the situation. Imagine yourself handling the challenge effectively, maintaining your composure, and feeling proud of your response.

5. **Develop a Support Plan:** Identify a support system you can reach out to when faced with unexpected challenges. Knowing you have someone to talk to can reduce the initial panic and help you strategize solutions.

6. **Create a 'Plan B':** For areas of your life where unexpected challenges frequently occur (e.g., work, family, health), develop a general 'Plan B' for how to cope when things don't go as planned. This might include alternative actions, resources, or help you can seek.

7. **Reflect and Learn:** After encountering an unexpected challenge, take time to reflect on your response. Consider what worked well and what you might do differently next time. Use this as a learning opportunity to improve your coping strategies.

Common pitfalls:

- **Overestimating the Challenge:** It's easy to magnify the severity of an unexpected situation. Try to maintain perspective and assess the challenge realistically.

- **Underestimating Your Ability to Cope:** Doubting your ability to handle unexpected challenges can increase anxiety. Trust in your resilience and problem-solving capabilities.

- **Neglecting Self-Care:** High stress levels can lead to neglecting self-care. Remember, maintaining your physical and emotional well-being is crucial for managing stress effectively.

Progress tracking:

Journaling: Keep a journal of unexpected challenges you face, your responses, and the outcomes. Over time, review your entries to identify improvements in your coping strategies and areas for further growth.

Stress and Anxiety Levels: Rate your stress and anxiety levels on a scale of 1-10 before and after applying these strategies to each unexpected challenge. Tracking these ratings can help you see your progress in managing reactions to stress.

12.3: Reprogramming Your Emotional Responses

Reprogramming your emotional responses involves a strategic approach to identifying, understanding, and altering the negative reactions that have become automatic over time. This process is crucial for anyone looking to manage everyday anxiety, stress, and triggers more effectively. By adopting specific techniques, you can learn to replace these negative reactions with more balanced and adaptive responses.

Cognitive Restructuring is a fundamental technique in this reprogramming process. It involves identifying the thoughts that lead to negative emotions and challenging them to assess their accuracy and helpfulness. For instance, if you find yourself thinking, "I can never do anything right," challenge this thought by asking, "Is it really true that I never do anything right?" By scrutinizing these thoughts, you can begin to replace them with more balanced ones, like, "Everyone makes mistakes, but I also have many successes."

Mindfulness and Awareness Practices play a significant role in reprogramming emotional responses. By becoming more aware of your thoughts and feelings without judgment, you can observe how certain thoughts lead to stress or anxiety. This awareness creates a space between stimulus and response, allowing you to choose how you react rather than being swept away by automatic negative reactions.

Emotional Regulation Techniques are essential tools. Techniques such as deep breathing, progressive muscle relaxation, and guided imagery can help calm the physiological arousal that often accompanies negative emotional responses. When you feel calmer, it's easier to access more rational and balanced ways of thinking about a situation.

Behavioral Experiments challenge you to test out the beliefs that underlie your negative emotional responses in real-world settings. If you're anxious about speaking up in meetings, for example, a behavioral experiment might involve making a small contribution to the next meeting and observing the outcome. Often, these experiments reveal that the feared outcome is less likely or catastrophic than imagined, helping to shift your emotional responses to similar situations in the future.

Positive Affirmation and Visualization can also aid in reprogramming your emotional responses. Regularly practicing affirmations that focus on your strengths and ability to handle stress can change your internal dialogue. Visualization, imagining yourself successfully navigating a situation that typically triggers a negative response, can also prepare you mentally and emotionally to handle real-life scenarios more adaptively.

Incorporating these techniques into your daily routine requires practice and patience. It's important to remember that changing deeply ingrained emotional responses doesn't happen overnight. However, with consistent application, these strategies can lead to significant improvements in how you respond to stress, anxiety, and everyday challenges, fostering a more balanced and adaptive emotional life.

Chapter 13: EMDR in Holistic Wellness

13.1: Combining EMDR with Grounding and Relaxation

Integrating Eye Movement Desensitization and Reprocessing (EMDR) with grounding and relaxation techniques offers a comprehensive approach to managing stress and enhancing emotional well-being. This combination leverages the strengths of each method to provide a more holistic and effective strategy for coping with daily pressures and emotional challenges. Grounding techniques, such as mindful breathing and sensory awareness exercises, help to anchor the individual in the present moment, reducing the intensity of stress and anxiety. These practices can be particularly beneficial in preparing the mind and body for EMDR sessions, creating a conducive state for processing and reprogramming negative emotional responses.

Mindful Breathing:

This involves focusing attention on the breath, observing its natural rhythm without trying to change it. This practice can help calm the mind and reduce stress levels, making it easier to engage in EMDR therapy. By incorporating mindful breathing before starting EMDR, individuals can enter a more relaxed state, facilitating the processing of traumatic memories.

Sensory Awareness Exercises:

Engaging the senses can powerfully ground an individual in the here and now, diverting attention away from distressing thoughts and feelings. Techniques might include holding a cold ice cube, feeling the texture of a fabric, or savoring the taste of a piece of fruit. These sensory experiences can serve as a bridge to EMDR, helping individuals become more present and less overwhelmed by emotional distress.

Visualization of a Safe Place:

Before embarking on EMDR therapy, individuals can benefit from visualizing a safe, peaceful place where they feel secure and calm. This mental imagery can create a psychological refuge, offering emotional protection during the processing of difficult memories. The safe place visualization can be revisited throughout the EMDR process to maintain a sense of safety and stability.

Positive Affirmations for Safety and Stability:

Repeating positive affirmations can reinforce a sense of personal safety and resilience. Affirmations such as "I am safe right now" or "I am in control of my healing" can be powerful tools for building confidence and emotional strength, complementing the EMDR process.

Creating a Personal Sanctuary:

Beyond the visualization of a safe place, individuals can also create a physical sanctuary—a dedicated space where they can engage in relaxation and grounding exercises. This space can serve as a supportive environment for both preparatory grounding techniques and post-EMDR reflection.

By combining EMDR with these grounding and relaxation techniques, individuals can enhance their capacity to manage stress and navigate emotional challenges with greater ease. This integrated approach not only facilitates the processing of traumatic memories but also strengthens overall emotional resilience, contributing to a more balanced and fulfilling life. Engaging regularly in these practices can empower individuals to maintain emotional equilibrium and foster a sense of inner peace, even in the face of life's inevitable stresses and strains.

13.2: Mindfulness and Meditation with EMDR

Integrating mindfulness and meditation with EMDR therapy offers a powerful combination for enhancing self-awareness and cultivating inner peace. Mindfulness, the practice of being fully present and engaged in the moment without judgment, complements the EMDR process by helping individuals become more attuned to their internal experiences. Meditation, on the other hand, provides a structured way to practice mindfulness, allowing for deeper exploration of thoughts and emotions, which can be particularly beneficial before and after EMDR sessions.

Mindful Breathing as a Foundation:

Start with mindful breathing exercises to establish a baseline of calm and presence. This technique involves focusing on the breath, noticing the inhalation and exhalation, and observing any bodily sensations without attempting to alter them. Mindful breathing can serve as a grounding exercise before beginning EMDR, preparing the mind and body for the therapeutic work ahead.

Body Scan Meditation for Increased Body Awareness:

Engage in a body scan meditation to heighten awareness of physical sensations throughout the body. This practice involves mentally scanning from the toes to the head, noting any discomfort, tension, or relaxation without trying to change the sensation. The body scan can reveal areas of stored stress or trauma, providing valuable insights for EMDR processing.

Observing Thoughts Meditation:

Practice meditation techniques that focus on observing thoughts as they arise and pass. This approach helps in developing a non-judgmental stance towards one's thoughts, which is crucial in EMDR therapy. By learning to observe thoughts without attachment, individuals can better process and reframe negative beliefs during EMDR sessions.

Loving-kindness Meditation to Foster Compassion:

Loving-kindness meditation can be particularly beneficial in the context of EMDR, as it encourages a compassionate and forgiving attitude towards oneself and others. This practice involves silently repeating phrases of goodwill and kindness towards oneself and extending these wishes to others. Cultivating compassion can enhance the therapeutic effects of EMDR by promoting emotional healing and resilience.

Integrating Meditation with EMDR Sessions:

Incorporate meditation practices into the EMDR protocol by beginning and ending sessions with a brief meditation. Starting with a grounding meditation can help clients feel more centered and prepared for the session, while concluding with a loving-kindness or gratitude meditation can reinforce positive outcomes and foster a sense of well-being.

Daily Mindfulness Practices:

Encourage the incorporation of mindfulness into daily life outside of therapy sessions. Simple practices like mindful eating, walking meditation, or mindful listening can enhance the benefits of EMDR by promoting a continuous state of awareness and presence. These practices help in consolidating the gains from EMDR therapy and support ongoing emotional and psychological growth.

By blending mindfulness and meditation with EMDR therapy, individuals can achieve a deeper level of healing and emotional freedom. These practices not only support the EMDR process but also contribute to a holistic approach to wellness, emphasizing the interconnectedness of mind, body, and spirit. Engaging in mindfulness and meditation regularly can empower individuals to navigate life's challenges with greater ease and resilience, fostering a lasting sense of peace and well-being.

13.3: Daily Practices for Mind-Body Balance

Establishing a daily routine that incorporates both physical exercises and mental health practices is essential for achieving and maintaining a mind-body balance. This holistic approach not only enhances the benefits of EMDR but also supports overall well-being. Here are some practical suggestions for integrating these practices into your daily life:

Physical Activities:

Regular physical exercise plays a critical role in reducing stress and improving mood. Activities such as walking, yoga, or swimming can be particularly beneficial. These exercises not only strengthen the body but also have a meditative effect on the mind, helping to clear away stress and anxiety. Aim for at least 30 minutes of moderate exercise most days of the week. If you're new to exercise, start with shorter durations and gradually increase as your fitness improves.

Mindful Movement:

Incorporate mindful movement practices such as tai chi or gentle yoga into your routine. These activities combine physical movement with mindfulness, enhancing body awareness and presence. By focusing on your movements and breathing, you can achieve a state of calm and centeredness that supports emotional processing.

Scheduled EMDR Self-Practice:

Dedicate time each day for EMDR self-help techniques, such as bilateral tapping or guided visualizations. These practices can be particularly effective when done in a quiet, comfortable space where you won't be disturbed. Morning sessions can help set a positive tone for the day, while evening practices can aid in processing the day's events and easing into restful sleep.

Breathing Exercises:

Diaphragmatic breathing, or deep breathing, is a powerful tool for managing stress and anxiety. Practice deep breathing for a few minutes at several points throughout the day. This can be especially helpful during moments of high stress or when preparing to engage in EMDR self-practice.

Mindfulness Meditation:

Daily meditation can significantly enhance your emotional well-being. Start with just a few minutes each day, gradually increasing the duration as you become more comfortable with the practice. Meditation apps or guided recordings can be helpful for beginners. The goal is to cultivate a state of non-judgmental awareness, allowing you to observe your thoughts and feelings without becoming overwhelmed by them.

Gratitude Journaling: End your day by writing down three things you're grateful for. This practice can shift your focus from stressors and challenges to positive aspects of your life, fostering a sense of contentment and well-being.

Nutrition and Hydration: Pay attention to your diet and make sure you're drinking enough water. Proper nutrition and hydration support brain function and emotional health, enhancing the effectiveness of EMDR and other mental health practices.

Quality Sleep: Prioritize getting enough sleep each night. Sleep is essential for emotional processing and recovery. Establish a relaxing bedtime routine and create a sleep-conducive environment to improve the quality of your rest.

By integrating these daily practices into your life, you can create a comprehensive wellness routine that supports both your physical and emotional health. Regular engagement in these activities can enhance the effectiveness of EMDR, helping you to achieve a greater sense of balance and well-being. Remember, consistency is key; even small, daily actions can lead to significant improvements over time.

Part 3: Strengthening Relationships and Resilience

Chapter 14: EMDR and Meaningful Relationships

14.1: How Trauma Impacts Relationships

Unresolved trauma can deeply affect the fabric of relationships, influencing communication, trust, and emotional connection in ways that might not be immediately apparent. Trauma, by its very nature, disrupts the normal processing of experiences, leaving individuals stuck in a loop of distressing memories and emotions. This can manifest in relationships through various, often subtle, behaviors and patterns.

Communication Challenges:

Individuals carrying the weight of unresolved trauma may find it difficult to articulate their thoughts and feelings. This can stem from a fear of not being understood or believed, or from the trauma itself, which might involve experiences of having their voice suppressed. Consequently, they might either withdraw, avoiding conversations about their feelings, or become overly defensive when topics related to their trauma are broached. This dynamic can create a barrier to open and honest communication, essential for healthy relationships.

Trust Issues:

Trust is foundational to any meaningful relationship, yet trauma can severely impair an individual's ability to trust others. Trauma survivors might perceive the world as unsafe and people as potential threats, leading to behaviors that push others away or create a fortress around their emotions. They might constantly seek reassurance from their partners or friends, or at the opposite end, become excessively self-reliant, refusing to depend on anyone. These trust issues can strain relationships, making it challenging to form deep, lasting connections.

Emotional Connection:

The emotional disconnect that often accompanies trauma can hinder the development of a strong emotional bond between individuals. Trauma can make it hard for people to access or express their emotions in a healthy way, leading to a flat affect or inappropriate emotional responses to situations. Partners or friends might feel like they are always on the outside, unable to reach in and truly connect with the trauma survivor. This disconnect can be frustrating and saddening for everyone involved, creating a sense of loneliness even in the presence of others.

Hyper-vigilance and Control:

Trauma can lead to a heightened state of alertness, where the individual is always on the lookout for danger. This hyper-vigilance can spill over into relationships, where the trauma survivor might attempt to control environments, situations, and even people, in an effort to feel safe. Such behaviors can be stifling for others, leading to conflict and resentment.

Intimacy Issues:

Both emotional and physical intimacy can be challenging for those with unresolved trauma. The vulnerability required for intimacy can be terrifying for trauma survivors, leading to avoidance of close physical contact or deep emotional sharing. This can leave partners feeling rejected and confused, damaging the intimacy that is vital for a healthy relationship.

Navigating Trauma in Relationships:

It's crucial for both the trauma survivor and their loved ones to recognize the impact of trauma on relationships. Seeking professional help through therapy can be a vital step in addressing and healing from trauma. Techniques such as EMDR can help individuals process their traumatic experiences in a safe and controlled environment, reducing their impact on the present.

For loved ones, educating themselves about trauma and its effects can foster a deeper understanding and patience. Open, non-judgmental communication about each person's needs and boundaries can help in navigating the complexities trauma introduces into relationships. Establishing a supportive environment where the trauma survivor feels safe to express their feelings and vulnerabilities without fear of judgment or rejection is essential.

Building a meaningful relationship in the shadow of trauma is undoubtedly challenging, but with empathy, patience, and professional support, it is possible to create a bond that is both healing and enriching.

14.2: Improving Communication with EMDR

EMDR therapy offers a unique approach to enhancing empathy and overcoming emotional barriers that hinder effective communication. By focusing on the reprocessing of distressing memories and negative beliefs, individuals can develop a deeper understanding of their own emotional responses and, in turn, become more attuned to the feelings of others. This heightened sense of empathy is crucial for building strong, meaningful relationships.

One of the key ways EMDR facilitates improved communication is through the identification and processing of past experiences that have led to the development of negative self-perceptions and beliefs about others. These might include feelings of inadequacy, fears of rejection, or deep-seated beliefs that one is unworthy of love and connection. Through targeted bilateral stimulation, individuals can begin to reprocess these memories, reducing their emotional impact and allowing for the adoption of more positive and constructive beliefs about oneself and others.

Moreover, EMDR therapy encourages the development of a more nuanced emotional vocabulary. As individuals process their experiences, they become more adept at identifying and articulating their feelings. This capability is essential for effective communication, as it enables individuals to express their needs, desires, and concerns more clearly, reducing the likelihood of misunderstandings and conflict.

The therapy also promotes resilience in the face of emotional triggers that may have previously led to withdrawal or conflict in relationships. By desensitizing these triggers, individuals can remain more emotionally present and engaged in their interactions with others, even when discussing sensitive or challenging topics. This resilience supports healthier and more adaptive communication patterns, fostering a sense of safety and trust within relationships.

Furthermore, EMDR's emphasis on the development of a 'safe space' during therapy sessions can be mirrored in interpersonal relationships. Individuals learn to create mental and emotional environments where open, honest communication is encouraged, and vulnerability is met with empathy and understanding. This safe space becomes a foundation for deepening connections and enhancing mutual understanding.

In addition to these direct benefits, EMDR therapy indirectly supports improved communication by reducing symptoms of anxiety and depression, which can be significant barriers to effective interpersonal interactions. As individuals experience relief from these symptoms, they often find it easier to engage socially, participate in meaningful conversations, and build supportive networks.

In practice, EMDR therapy equips individuals with the tools to approach conversations with a sense of curiosity and openness, rather than defensiveness or fear. This shift in perspective is critical for overcoming communication barriers and building relationships based on mutual respect and understanding. Through the therapeutic process, individuals learn to listen actively, respond empathetically, and express themselves authentically, transforming their interactions and relationships in profound and lasting ways.

14.3: Exercises to Strengthen Connections and Empathy

Exercise 1: Building Empathy through Active Listening

Objective: To enhance your ability to understand and connect with others by practicing active listening, a fundamental component of empathy. This exercise aims to improve your relationships through deeper emotional understanding and communication.

Step-by-step instructions:

1. **Choose a Partner:** Select a friend, family member, or colleague who is willing to participate in this exercise with you. Explain the purpose of the exercise to ensure they are comfortable and willing to share openly.

2. **Set Aside Distraction-Free Time:** Arrange a time and place where you can talk without interruptions. Turn off all digital devices or put them on silent mode to ensure full attention to the conversation.

3. **Establish the Topic:** Ask your partner to share something important to them or something they have been experiencing lately. It could be a personal challenge, a success story, or simply how their day went.

4. **Practice Active Listening:** As your partner speaks, focus entirely on what they are saying. Avoid the urge to think about your response while they are talking. Nod your head, maintain eye contact, and use verbal cues like "I see" or "Go on" to show you are engaged.

5. **Reflect and Clarify:** After your partner has finished speaking, reflect back what you heard in your own words. For example, "It sounds like you felt really proud when..." This step ensures you have correctly understood their message and gives them a chance to clarify if needed.

6. **Respond Empathetically:** Once you have fully understood their perspective, respond with empathy. Acknowledge their feelings and offer support. For instance, "That must have been really difficult for you" or "I'm so happy to hear you succeeded."

7. **Switch Roles:** After the first part of the exercise, switch roles and repeat the process with you sharing and your partner listening.

8. **Discuss the Experience:** Once both of you have shared and listened, discuss how the exercise felt. Talk about what you learned from the experience and how it might affect your communication going forward.

Common pitfalls:

- **Interrupting:** Cutting off the speaker not only disrupts their train of thought but also signals that their words are not valued. Resist the urge to interrupt, even if you have something important to add.

- **Planning Your Response While Listening:** This can prevent you from fully understanding the speaker's message and emotions. Focus fully on listening until they have finished speaking.

- **Judging or Offering Unsolicited Advice:** This exercise is about understanding and empathy, not about solving problems unless advice is specifically requested.

Progress tracking:

Journaling: After each active listening session, jot down your reflections. Note what you found challenging, any new insights into your partner's feelings or thoughts, and how the experience affected your emotional connection.

Feedback: Ask for feedback from your partner on how heard and understood they felt during the exercise. Use this feedback to improve your active listening skills.

Emotional Awareness: Pay attention to any changes in your emotional awareness and empathy levels as you continue practicing active listening in your daily interactions. Note any shifts in your relationships or communication style.

Exercise 2: Strengthening Connections with Shared Experiences

Objective: To foster deeper connections and empathy within personal and professional relationships by sharing and reflecting on personal experiences with others. This exercise aims to enhance understanding, trust, and emotional intimacy between individuals.

Step-by-step instructions:

1. **Choose a Partner or Group:** Select a trusted individual or a small group of people with whom you feel comfortable sharing personal stories and experiences.

2. **Set a Comfortable Environment:** Arrange a quiet, relaxed setting free from distractions where everyone can speak and listen comfortably. Ensure all participants agree to confidentiality and respect for each other's stories.

3. **Select a Theme:** Agree on a broad theme for sharing, such as challenges overcome, moments of change, or experiences of joy. The theme should be wide enough to allow personal interpretation but focused enough to maintain a cohesive discussion.

4. **Share Personal Stories:** Take turns sharing personal stories related to the chosen theme. Encourage each person to speak without interruption, sharing as much or as little as they feel comfortable.

5. **Reflect and Respond:** After each story, allow time for reflection and responses from the group. Responses should focus on expressing empathy, asking open-ended questions to understand more deeply, and sharing any similar feelings or experiences, if appropriate.

6. **Express Gratitude:** Once everyone has shared, close the session by expressing gratitude for the openness and support. Acknowledge the courage it takes to share personal stories and the value of the connections strengthened through this process.

7. **Discuss Insights:** Optionally, discuss any new insights or perspectives gained through the exercise. Reflect on how the exercise has impacted your understanding and empathy towards each other.

Common pitfalls:

- **Dominating the Conversation:** Be mindful not to dominate the conversation. Ensure everyone has equal opportunity to share and respond.

- **Offering Unsolicited Advice:** Focus on listening and empathizing rather than offering unsolicited advice or trying to "fix" the situation.

- **Judgment or Criticism:** Avoid judgment or criticism of others' experiences. The goal is to foster understanding and empathy, not to evaluate the experiences shared.

Progress tracking:

Journaling: Participants may choose to journal about their feelings and insights after the exercise. Reflecting on the stories shared and the emotions they evoked can deepen the exercise's impact.

Follow-Up Discussions: Arrange follow-up discussions to explore any ongoing changes in perceptions or relationships as a result of the exercise. This can help solidify the connections and understandings developed.

Exercise 3: Enhancing Understanding through Perspective-Taking

Objective: To foster deeper understanding and empathy in relationships through the practice of perspective-taking, enabling individuals to connect on a more meaningful level and navigate interpersonal interactions with greater sensitivity and awareness.

Step-by-step instructions:

1. **Select a Recent Interaction:** Think of a recent conversation or interaction with someone that left you feeling puzzled, upset, or disconnected.

2. **Recount Their Perspective:** Write down or verbally recount the interaction from the other person's point of view. Focus on what they might have been thinking and feeling, even if it differs greatly from your own perspective.

3. **Identify Emotions:** Try to identify the emotions the other person might have been experiencing during the interaction. Consider factors like their tone of voice, body language, and choice of words to infer their emotional state.

4. **Reflect on Background Factors:** Consider any background factors that might influence the other person's perspective, such as their personal history, cultural background, or current stressors in their life.

5. **Compare Perspectives:** Compare your original perspective of the interaction with the new perspective you've considered. Note any differences in how you now understand the situation and the other person's possible intentions and feelings.

6. **Plan a Follow-up:** Based on your new understanding, plan a follow-up interaction with the person. Aim to express your newfound perspective and seek clarification on any points you may have misunderstood.

7. **Engage in Active Listening:** During your follow-up, practice active listening. Focus fully on what the other person is saying without planning your response. Ask open-ended questions to deepen your understanding of their perspective.

8. **Reflect on the Outcome:** After the follow-up interaction, take time to reflect on any changes in your relationship dynamic. Note any improvements in understanding, empathy, and connection.

Common pitfalls:

- **Assuming You Already Know:** One common pitfall is assuming you already know what the other person thinks or feels without truly considering their perspective.

- **Neglecting Non-Verbal Cues:** Failing to consider non-verbal cues in your analysis can lead to a misunderstanding of the other person's emotions and intentions.

- **Projection:** Avoid projecting your own feelings and reactions onto the other person. Remember, their experience and emotional response may be very different from your own.

Progress tracking:

Journaling: Keep a journal of your attempts at perspective-taking. Note the situation, your initial thoughts, the perspective you explored, and the outcome of any follow-up interaction.

Feedback: Seek feedback from the person you had the interaction with, if appropriate. Ask if your understanding of their perspective was accurate and what you could do to improve your empathy and understanding.

- **Reflect on Growth:** Periodically review your journal entries to assess your growth in perspective-taking and empathy. Note any patterns in misunderstandings and how your relationships have improved through this practice.

Chapter 15: Building Emotional Resilience

15.1: Understanding and Embracing Resilience

Building emotional resilience is akin to constructing a fortress within oneself, a stronghold that shelters and empowers an individual to face life's tumultuous storms with courage and stability. Emotional resilience is the bedrock upon which one can lean during times of distress, enabling a bounce-back with greater wisdom and strength. It is not merely about surviving the adversities but thriving amidst them, transforming challenges into stepping stones for growth. This inner fortitude is essential for navigating the complexities of modern life, where change is the only constant and stressors lurk around every corner.

To cultivate this resilience, it is imperative to develop a toolkit of coping strategies and techniques that can be deployed when confronted with stress or change. First and foremost, **mindfulness practice** stands out as a powerful tool. By fostering an awareness of the present moment, without judgment, individuals can gain insights into their thought patterns and emotional responses, allowing for a more measured and controlled reaction to stressors. Mindfulness can be cultivated through meditation, deep breathing exercises, or simply by engaging fully with the present activity.

Another cornerstone of building resilience is **emotional regulation**. This involves understanding and managing one's emotions, rather than being led by them. Techniques such as cognitive reappraisal, where one reframes a negative situation into a more positive or neutral light, can significantly alter emotional responses, reducing feelings of anxiety and depression.

Social support also plays a crucial role in enhancing resilience. Strong, healthy relationships provide a buffer against the vicissitudes of life. Knowing that one has a supportive network to rely on can make facing challenges less daunting. It is important to cultivate these relationships, not only for the support they provide but also for the opportunity they offer to support others, which in itself can be a resilience-building experience.

Self-efficacy, the belief in one's ability to influence events and outcomes in one's life, is another critical element. Building self-efficacy can be achieved through setting and achieving small goals, thus providing evidence of one's competence and bolstering confidence in one's abilities.

Lastly, **self-care** is paramount. Regular physical activity, adequate sleep, and a nutritious diet all contribute to a strong physical foundation that supports emotional and psychological well-being. Engaging in hobbies and activities that bring joy and relaxation can also replenish one's emotional reserves.

Incorporating these practices into daily life does not mean that one will never face difficulty or distress. However, it ensures that when challenges arise, the resources and strategies to manage them effectively are at hand. Building emotional resilience is an ongoing process, a journey of self-discovery and growth that enhances one's capacity to navigate life's ups and downs with grace and strength. Through the deliberate application of these techniques, individuals can fortify their emotional resilience, transforming adversity into opportunity and leading a more fulfilling, balanced life.

15.2 Techniques for Facing Challenges with Stability

Adopting a proactive approach to **problem-solving** is another key technique in maintaining emotional stability. When faced with a challenge, breaking it down into manageable parts can make it less overwhelming. This method involves identifying the problem, brainstorming possible solutions, evaluating the pros and cons of each, and then implementing the most viable solution. This structured approach not only provides a clear path forward but also instills a sense of control and competence.

Perspective-shifting is a powerful tool for emotional resilience. It involves consciously choosing to view a situation from a different angle or through a more positive lens. For instance, instead of seeing a failure as a setback, one can view it as an opportunity to learn and grow. This doesn't mean ignoring the negative aspects but rather acknowledging them without allowing them to dominate your thoughts and emotions.

Setting boundaries is crucial for emotional stability. It's important to recognize and communicate your limits in both personal and professional relationships. This can prevent feelings of resentment or burnout, which often arise from overcommitment or having your boundaries disregarded. Learning to say no, or not now, is a skill that protects your emotional energy and allows you to focus on what truly matters to you.

Practicing gratitude can significantly enhance emotional resilience. Regularly acknowledging and appreciating the good in your life, even during tough times, can shift your focus from what's lacking or problematic to what's abundant and right. Keeping a gratitude journal or simply reflecting on three things you're grateful for each day can foster a more positive and resilient mindset.

Seeking support from friends, family, or professionals is essential when facing difficult situations. Sharing your challenges with others can provide new insights, practical advice, or simply the comfort of knowing you're not alone. Support networks can also offer encouragement and remind you of your strengths and past successes, bolstering your confidence and resilience.

Engaging in regular physical activity is a well-documented strategy for managing stress and enhancing mood. Exercise releases endorphins, which have natural stress-relieving and mood-boosting effects. Whether it's a brisk walk, yoga, or more vigorous activities, finding a form of exercise that you enjoy and can consistently engage in is a valuable component of your emotional resilience toolkit.

Developing a mindfulness practice can help you stay grounded in the present moment, reducing worries about the future or ruminations on the past. Techniques such as deep breathing, meditation, or even mindful walking can help calm the mind and body, making it easier to approach challenges with a clear and focused mind.

Creating a self-care routine that includes activities and practices that you enjoy and find relaxing can replenish your emotional and physical energy. This might involve reading, taking baths, engaging in hobbies, or spending time in nature. Prioritizing self-care is not selfish; it's a necessary aspect of maintaining your well-being and resilience.

By integrating these techniques into your daily life, you can enhance your ability to face challenges with stability and confidence. Each strategy contributes to a foundation of emotional resilience, enabling you to navigate life's ups and downs with greater ease and grace.

15.3: Turning Stress into Growth Opportunities

Transforming stress into opportunities for growth and transformation involves a shift in perception and the adoption of strategies that leverage challenging moments as catalysts for personal development and emotional evolution. This process begins with the recognition that stress, while often perceived negatively, can serve as a powerful motivator and teacher, guiding us toward areas in our lives that require attention, change, or development.

Reframing Stressful Situations is a critical first step. It involves altering your perspective on stressors, viewing them not as insurmountable obstacles but as challenges that hold the potential for growth. By asking yourself what lessons can be learned or what strengths can be developed in response to a stressful situation, you begin to shift from a mindset of victimhood to one of empowerment.

Embracing a Growth Mindset is essential for seeing stress as an opportunity. A growth mindset, as opposed to a fixed mindset, thrives on challenge and sees failure not as evidence of unintelligence but as a heartening springboard for growth and for stretching our existing abilities. When faced with stress, individuals with a growth mindset are more likely to engage in adaptive behaviors, seeking solutions and learning from the experience rather than feeling defeated.

Setting Realistic Goals and Expectations helps in managing stress by providing clear direction and purpose. Goals give us something to work toward and help focus our energies constructively, turning stress into a driving force for achieving personal and professional aspirations. It's important, however, to ensure these goals are realistic and achievable; setting the bar too high can lead to increased stress and feelings of inadequacy.

Developing Problem-Solving Skills is another way to transform stress into opportunity. When confronted with a stressful situation, having a methodical approach to identifying solutions can not only reduce the immediate stress but also build confidence in your ability to handle future challenges. This might involve breaking the problem down into smaller, more manageable parts, identifying various solutions, and weighing their pros and cons.

Seeking Learning Opportunities in Every Situation encourages continuous personal development. Each stressful situation holds the potential for learning something new about ourselves, others, or the world around us. Whether it's developing a new skill, gaining deeper emotional insight, or simply learning what strategies do not work, every challenge offers valuable lessons.

Practicing Mindfulness and Presence can transform the experience of stress. By staying present with our stress without judgment, we can observe our reactions to it and learn from them. This practice can reveal underlying patterns or triggers of stress, offering insights into how we might address these root causes rather than just the symptoms.

Building a Supportive Network is crucial for turning stress into an opportunity for growth. Sharing your experiences with trusted friends, family members, or colleagues can provide new perspectives, emotional support, and practical advice. Sometimes, just the act of verbalizing your stress can diminish its power and help clarify the way forward.

Maintaining Physical Well-being plays a significant role in how we perceive and respond to stress. Regular physical activity, adequate rest, and a nutritious diet can enhance our overall resilience, making us better equipped to view stress as an opportunity rather than a threat.

Cultivating Emotional Intelligence (EI) is key to using stress beneficially. EI involves the ability to recognize, understand, and manage our own emotions, as well as the emotions of others. By developing EI, we can navigate stressful situations more effectively, using them as opportunities to practice emotional regulation, empathy, and interpersonal skills.

Implementing Stress Reduction Techniques such as deep breathing, meditation, or yoga can help lower the physiological and psychological impacts of stress, creating space for reflection and growth. These practices can also enhance our capacity for resilience, enabling us to bounce back from stressors more quickly and with greater insight.

Incorporating these strategies into your life does not eliminate stress but transforms your relationship with it. By viewing stress through the lens of opportunity, you can harness its energy to propel you forward, turning potential obstacles into stepping stones for personal and emotional development.

Part 4: Growth and Transformation

Chapter 16. Daily Self-Care Routine with EMDR

16.1: Blending EMDR with Journaling and Gratitude

Integrating Eye Movement Desensitization and Reprocessing (EMDR) techniques with journaling and expressions of gratitude can significantly enhance your daily self-care routine, offering a multifaceted approach to emotional well-being. This method not only leverages the therapeutic power of EMDR but also taps into the reflective and positive aspects of journaling and gratitude practices. Here, we delve into the specifics of combining these practices effectively.

Journaling as a Companion to EMDR

Journaling can serve as a powerful tool to complement EMDR therapy. After an EMDR session, whether guided by a professional or through self-administered techniques, journaling can help consolidate the insights and emotional shifts experienced during the session. Writing about your thoughts and feelings can provide a form of externalization, allowing you to process and understand your emotions more deeply. To integrate journaling with EMDR, consider the following steps:

1. **Post-EMDR Reflection:**
   Immediately after your EMDR practice, spend a few minutes writing about the experience. Note any memories, sensations, or emotions that surfaced. This can help anchor the therapeutic effects of the session.

2. **Daily Emotional Check-in:**
   Use your journal to track your emotional state each day. This can help you identify patterns or triggers in your life that may need further attention with EMDR techniques.

3. **Gratitude Integration:**
   At the end of each journal entry, list three things you are grateful for. This practice can shift your focus from negative thoughts and emotions to positive aspects of your life, reinforcing the positive belief systems strengthened by EMDR.

Gratitude Practices to Enhance EMDR

Gratitude exercises can significantly amplify the benefits of EMDR therapy by promoting a positive mindset and emotional resilience. Incorporating gratitude into your EMDR routine can be done in several ways:

- **Gratitude List:** Make a daily habit of writing down things you are grateful for. These can be as simple as a warm cup of coffee in the morning or as significant as the support of a loved one. This practice can be particularly powerful when done right after an EMDR session, as it helps to solidify any positive shifts in perspective.

- **Gratitude Meditation:** Combine EMDR bilateral stimulation, such as tapping or eye movements, with a gratitude meditation. Focus on a feeling of gratitude while engaging in the bilateral stimulation to enhance the emotional and neurological benefits of both practices.

- **Gratitude Letters:** Write letters of gratitude to people in your life, expressing appreciation for their presence and actions. This does not only foster positive relationships but also helps you internalize a sense of gratitude and abundance, which can be therapeutic in the context of EMDR.

Creating a Routine

To effectively blend EMDR techniques with journaling and gratitude practices, consistency is key. Establish a routine that incorporates these practices into your daily life. This might look like dedicating time each morning or evening to engage in EMDR self-help techniques, followed by journaling and a brief gratitude exercise. Over time, this integrated approach can lead to profound changes in your emotional well-being, helping you to manage stress, overcome anxiety, and foster meaningful relationships with a sense of emotional freedom.

16.2: Checklist to Track EMDR Progress

To ensure you're making the most of your EMDR self-care routine and tracking your progress effectively, consider incorporating the following checklist into your daily or weekly practices. This tool is designed to help you monitor your use of EMDR techniques and gauge your personal development over time. By regularly reviewing and completing this checklist, you can identify areas of strength and those needing further attention, facilitating a more tailored and effective approach to your emotional well-being.

EMDR Progress Tracking Checklist

1. **Date and Time of Practice:**
   Record when you performed your EMDR self-care routine. This helps in establishing a consistent practice schedule.

2. **Techniques Used:**
   Note down the specific EMDR techniques you employed, such as bilateral tapping, eye movements, or guided visualizations. This will help you identify which methods are most effective for you.

3. **Duration of Practice:**
   Keep track of how long each session lasts. Aim for consistency but adjust as needed based on your daily schedule and emotional state.

4. **Emotional State Before Practice:**
   Rate your emotional state on a scale from 1 to 10 before beginning your EMDR session. This provides a baseline for assessing the impact of your practice.

5. **Trigger or Issue Addressed:**
   Briefly describe the specific trigger, thought, or issue you focused on during your EMDR practice. This aids in tracking the types of challenges you're working through over time.

6. **Emotional State After Practice:**
   Rate your emotional state again after completing your EMDR session. Comparing this rating with your pre-practice state can offer insight into the immediate effects of your efforts.

7. **Insights Gained:**
   Jot down any insights, revelations, or shifts in perspective you experienced. Acknowledging these moments can reinforce the positive outcomes of your practice.

8. **Areas for Further Attention:**
   Identify any emotions, triggers, or issues that continue to challenge you or that emerged during your practice. This can guide your focus in future sessions.

9. **Gratitude Moment:**
   Reflect on at least one aspect of your life you feel grateful for at the moment. Integrating gratitude with EMDR enhances the positive impact on your emotional health.

10. **Overall Progress Note:**
    Summarize your overall sense of progress and any changes in your emotional well-being since beginning your EMDR self-care routine. Recognizing growth, even in small increments, can be incredibly motivating.

11. **Adjustments for Next Session:**

Based on your session and the insights gained, note any adjustments you plan to make for your next practice. This might include trying a new technique, focusing on a different issue, or adjusting the length of your session.

By maintaining this checklist, you're not only committing to your emotional health but also empowering yourself with concrete data on your journey toward emotional freedom and resilience. Remember, the path to well-being is a personal one, and what matters most is finding the rhythm and practices that resonate with you.

Chapter 17. Achieving Emotional Freedom

17.1: Transforming Negative Experiences into Resources

Transforming negative experiences into positive resources involves a deliberate shift in perspective and the application of specific strategies to reframe and repurpose past adversities. This process is not about denying the pain or difficulty of these experiences but about recognizing their potential to contribute to personal growth, resilience, and a deeper understanding of oneself and the world. Here are practical steps to achieve this transformation:

1. **Identify the Negative Experience:**
   Begin by acknowledging the negative experience. This could be a traumatic event, a series of challenges, or even a pattern of thinking that has contributed to your current state of distress. Recognition is the first step towards transformation.

2. **Analyze the Impact:**
Reflect on how this experience has affected your life, beliefs, and behaviors. Understanding the impact allows you to see the areas in which growth is needed and possible.

3. **Seek the Lessons:**
Every challenge carries a lesson. Ask yourself what you can learn from this experience. Perhaps it taught you resilience, compassion, or the importance of setting boundaries. Identifying the lesson helps shift the focus from victimhood to empowerment.

4. **Reframe the Narrative:**
Change the story you tell yourself about the experience. Instead of viewing it as a purely negative event that happened to you, try to see it as a pivotal moment that contributed to your personal development. This reframing can alter your emotional response to the memory.

5. **Develop New Beliefs:**
Based on the lessons learned, cultivate new, positive beliefs about yourself and your ability to handle challenges. Replace thoughts like "I can't handle this" with "I can learn from my experiences and grow stronger."

6. **Apply the Lessons:**
Use the insights gained to inform your future actions and decisions. If you've learned the importance of self-care, make it a priority in your life. If you've discovered inner strength, remind yourself of this power when faced with new challenges.

7. **Share Your Insights:**
Helping others by sharing your story and the lessons you've learned can be incredibly therapeutic and empowering. It not only reinforces your own growth but can also inspire resilience and hope in others.

8. **Practice Gratitude:**
Cultivate a habit of gratitude, even for the challenges that have shaped you. Gratitude shifts your focus from what you've lost or endured to the strength, wisdom, and compassion you've gained.

9. **Integrate the Experience into Your Identity:**
Accept that this experience is part of your story but does not define you. It has contributed to your growth, resilience, and the unique perspective you bring to your life and relationships.

10. **Seek Professional Support if Needed:**
Sometimes, the process of transforming negative experiences into positive resources can be overwhelming. If you find it difficult to navigate this process on your own, consider seeking the support of a therapist or counselor who can guide you through it.

By actively engaging in this process, you can begin to view your past not as a series of obstacles but as a valuable source of strength, wisdom, and motivation. This shift in perspective is not only healing but also empowering, opening up new possibilities for personal development and fulfillment.

17.2: Cultivating Growth and Resilience Mindset

Developing a mindset for growth and resilience requires a conscious effort to foster attitudes and behaviors that support personal development and emotional strength. This mindset is not innate; it is cultivated through practice and intention. Here are strategies to nurture a growth and resilience mindset:

Embrace Challenges as Opportunities:

View challenges not as insurmountable obstacles but as opportunities to learn and grow. Each difficulty you encounter is a chance to develop problem-solving skills and resilience. When faced with a challenge, ask yourself, "What can I learn from this?" and "How can this experience make me stronger?"

Practice Self-Compassion:

Be kind and understanding toward yourself, especially in times of failure or when confronting personal shortcomings. Recognize that perfection is unattainable and that mistakes are part of the learning process. Treat yourself with the same compassion you would offer a friend in a similar situation.

Set Realistic Goals:

Goal setting is crucial for personal growth, but it's important to set achievable, realistic goals. Break larger goals into smaller, manageable tasks to avoid feeling overwhelmed. Celebrate each small victory to maintain motivation and a sense of progress.

Cultivate a Positive Social Network:

Surround yourself with supportive individuals who encourage your growth and resilience. Positive relationships provide emotional support, offer new perspectives, and can inspire you to achieve your best. Conversely, minimize time with those who drain your energy or discourage your aspirations.

Adopt a Flexible Mindset:

Be open to change and willing to adapt your strategies when necessary. Flexibility is a key component of resilience, allowing you to navigate life's uncertainties more effectively. When a plan doesn't work out, consider alternative approaches rather than giving up.

Focus on Continuous Learning:

Commit to lifelong learning, whether through formal education, self-study, or experiential learning. Embrace curiosity and seek out new knowledge and skills. This not only enhances your personal and professional life but also contributes to a sense of fulfillment and self-efficacy.

Practice Mindfulness and Gratitude:

Mindfulness helps you stay present and engaged, reducing stress and enhancing emotional regulation. Gratitude shifts your focus from what's lacking to what's abundant in your life, fostering positivity and resilience. Incorporate mindfulness and gratitude practices into your daily routine.

Reflect Regularly:

Regular reflection allows you to assess your progress, understand your emotions, and recognize patterns in your thoughts and behaviors. Use journaling as a tool for reflection, helping you to clarify your thoughts, solve problems more efficiently, and track your growth over time.

Seek Feedback Constructively:

Feedback, even when critical, is valuable for personal growth. Approach feedback with an open mind, considering it as a resource for learning rather than a personal attack. Use it to refine your strategies and improve your skills.

Celebrate Effort, Not Just Outcome:

Recognize and celebrate the effort you put into pursuing your goals, regardless of the outcome. This reinforces the value of hard work and perseverance, key components of a growth mindset.

By integrating these strategies into your life, you can develop a mindset that embraces growth and resilience, enabling you to navigate life's challenges with confidence and optimism. This mindset is not only about overcoming adversity but also about seizing opportunities for personal development and emotional well-being.

Part 5: Additional Resources

Chapter 18: Digital Tools for EMDR Practice

18.1: Apps for Bilateral Stimulation and Mindfulness

In the realm of digital tools for bilateral stimulation and mindfulness, there is a plethora of applications designed to support individuals in their journey toward emotional well-being. These tools leverage technology to make Eye Movement Desensitization and Reprocessing (EMDR) more accessible and user-friendly, allowing users to engage in therapeutic practices from the comfort of their homes or while on the go. Here, we delve into several noteworthy apps and digital resources that stand out for their effectiveness in providing bilateral stimulation and mindfulness exercises.

Bilateral Stimulation Apps:

1. **EMDR Relief:** This app offers a range of customizable features for bilateral stimulation, including adjustable speeds and patterns of light movement. Users can select the type of stimulation that best suits their needs, making it a versatile tool for self-help EMDR practice.

2. **Virtual EMDR:** Designed to simulate the EMDR therapy process, this app provides guided sessions with visual and auditory stimulation. It includes a variety of settings to tailor the experience, including different sounds and visual patterns to engage both hemispheres of the brain.

3. **Bilateral Brainwave:** Incorporating binaural beats, this app aims to enhance bilateral stimulation through auditory means. It offers a selection of sounds designed to promote relaxation and mental balance, suitable for individuals looking to combine EMDR techniques with meditation.

Mindfulness and Meditation Apps:

1. **Headspace:** Renowned for its user-friendly interface and comprehensive meditation library, Headspace offers guided meditations on a wide range of topics, including stress management, anxiety relief, and personal growth. Its sessions vary in length, making it easy to incorporate mindfulness into any schedule.

2. **Calm:** This app provides an extensive collection of meditation sessions, sleep stories, and music tracks designed to foster relaxation and mindfulness. Calm stands out for its focus on improving sleep quality, a common challenge for individuals dealing with stress and anxiety.

3. **Insight Timer:** With a vast library of free meditations, Insight Timer caters to users at all levels of meditation practice. It features guided sessions by renowned mindfulness experts and allows users to customize their meditation experience with different background sounds and durations.

Combining Bilateral Stimulation with Mindfulness:

For those interested in integrating bilateral stimulation techniques with mindfulness practices, exploring apps that offer both functionalities can be beneficial. Some apps provide guided EMDR sessions that incorporate mindfulness and relaxation exercises as part of the therapy process. This holistic approach supports the brain's natural healing mechanisms by combining the therapeutic benefits of EMDR with the calming effects of mindfulness.

When selecting an app or digital tool, consider factors such as ease of use, customization options, and the variety of features offered. It's essential to choose a resource that aligns with your personal preferences and therapeutic goals. Additionally, while these digital tools can be incredibly supportive, they are not a substitute for professional therapy. Individuals with severe or complex mental health concerns should seek guidance from a qualified EMDR therapist.

Incorporating digital tools for bilateral stimulation and mindfulness into your self-care routine can enhance your mental well-being and support your journey toward emotional freedom. By leveraging these resources, you can access therapeutic techniques that foster resilience, emotional regulation, and personal growth.

Chapter 19. Choosing an EMDR Therapist

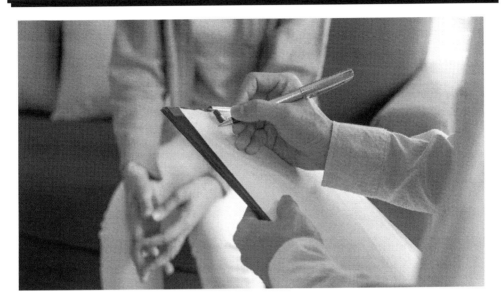

19.1: What to Look for in a Qualified Therapist

When seeking a qualified Eye Movement Desensitization and Reprocessing (EMDR) therapist, it is crucial to consider several factors to ensure that the professional you choose is well-equipped to guide you through the therapeutic process effectively. Here are the key criteria to look for:

1. **Certification and Training**:
   Ensure the therapist is certified by a recognized EMDR organization. This certification indicates that they have completed the requisite training and have a solid understanding of the EMDR process. Additionally, inquire about any advanced training they may have undergone, as this can provide deeper insights into their expertise and commitment to their practice.

2. **Experience**:
   Experience is a significant factor when choosing a therapist. Look for a professional who has a proven track record of working with clients with issues similar to yours. Ask about the number of years they have been practicing EMDR and the variety of conditions they have treated. Experienced therapists are likely to have encountered a wide range of scenarios and will be better prepared to handle complex cases.

3. **Specialization**:
   While EMDR is used to treat various conditions, some therapists may specialize in specific areas, such as anxiety, PTSD, or depression. If you are seeking therapy for a particular issue, finding a therapist with a specialization in that area can be beneficial. Their focused expertise can offer more tailored and effective treatment strategies.

4. **Approach and Techniques**:
   Each therapist may have a unique approach to EMDR therapy. Discuss their methodology and the techniques they employ during sessions. Understanding their approach can help you gauge if it aligns with your preferences and if you would feel comfortable with their style of therapy.

5. **Professional Affiliations**:
   Membership in professional EMDR associations or other mental health organizations can be a good indicator of a therapist's dedication to their practice and to staying updated with the latest developments in the field. These affiliations often require members to adhere to specific ethical standards and engage in continuous education.

6. **Client-Therapist Fit**:
   The therapeutic relationship is a critical component of effective therapy. It's important to choose a therapist with whom you feel comfortable and safe. Initial consultations can be a great way to assess this fit. Pay attention to how they communicate, their level of empathy, and whether they provide a space where you feel heard and understood.

7. **Feedback and Outcomes**:
   While confidentiality agreements may limit the specifics a therapist can share about past clients, asking about general outcomes and how feedback is incorporated into their practice can offer insights into their effectiveness and adaptability. A therapist who is open to feedback and willing to adjust their methods to better suit their clients' needs is likely to provide a more personalized and effective therapeutic experience.

8. **Logistics**:
   Practical considerations such as location, session availability, and insurance coverage also play a significant role in choosing a therapist. Ensure their logistical arrangements align with your needs to maintain consistency in therapy without added stress.

By carefully considering these criteria, you can make a more informed decision when selecting an EMDR therapist. Remember, the goal is to find a professional who not only meets the technical qualifications but also provides a therapeutic environment where you feel supported and empowered to work through your challenges.

19.2: Questions to Ask During the First Session

1. **How do you handle setbacks during therapy?**

It's important to understand the therapist's approach to challenges or slower-than-expected progress. Their response can offer insights into their resilience, adaptability, and support systems in place for clients who may find themselves struggling or not advancing as anticipated in their therapeutic journey.

2. **Can you describe a case similar to mine that you have worked on, and what were the outcomes?**

While confidentiality will prevent them from sharing detailed personal information, therapists can generally discuss case types and outcomes. This question helps gauge their experience with similar issues and their success in helping others overcome them.

3. **How do you measure progress in therapy?**

Knowing the metrics or signs a therapist looks for can help set clear expectations for your therapy journey. It also highlights their focus on goal-setting and accountability in the therapeutic process.

4. What is your availability for sessions, and how do you handle emergencies or crises?

This question addresses logistical concerns but also tests their commitment to client support outside scheduled sessions. It's crucial to know you have a reliable point of contact in urgent situations.

5. How do you incorporate feedback from clients into your therapy approach?

A therapist who is open to and encourages feedback is likely to be collaborative and adaptive, traits that are beneficial in a therapeutic relationship.

6. What are your views on medication vs. therapy for treatment?

Understanding their perspective on medication can inform you about their treatment philosophy and how it aligns with your preferences or needs.

7. How do you stay updated with the latest EMDR research and techniques?

A therapist committed to their professional development is likely to provide the most current and effective treatment options.

8. What role do you see my family or significant others playing in my therapy?

This question can uncover their approach to systemic or relational aspects of your challenges and whether they consider involving your support network as part of the treatment plan.

9. How long do you typically work with clients?

While the duration of therapy can vary widely depending on individual needs and goals, their answer can provide a general expectation and if they tend towards short-term or long-term therapy.

10. What do you find most rewarding about working with clients in EMDR therapy?

This question offers a glimpse into their passion and commitment to their work, which can be a strong indicator of their dedication to helping clients heal and grow.

11. How do you define success in therapy, and how can we work together to achieve it?

Success can look different for everyone, and a therapist's ability to articulate this and collaborate on a shared vision for success is key to a productive therapeutic relationship.

12. What is your policy on confidentiality and privacy?

Understanding the boundaries of confidentiality, including any exceptions, is crucial for establishing trust and safety within the therapeutic relationship.

Chapter 20: Guided Exercises for Everyday Life

20.1: Managing Daily Stress and Overwhelm

Exercise: Quick Breathing and Tapping for Stress Reduction

Objective: To quickly reduce stress and improve mental calmness through a combination of breathing and tapping techniques, providing immediate relief in moments of overwhelm or anxiety.

Step-by-step instructions:

1. **Find a Comfortable Position:** Sit or stand in a place where you can remain undisturbed for a few minutes. Ensure your posture is relaxed yet upright.

2. **Focus on Your Breath:** Close your eyes and take a deep breath in through your nose, counting to four. Hold your breath for a count of four, then slowly exhale through your mouth for a count of six. Repeat this breathing pattern three times to prepare your body and mind for the tapping exercise.

3. **Begin Tapping:** Using the fingertips of one hand, start tapping gently but firmly on the side of your other hand, specifically on the fleshy part below the thumb (known as the karate chop point). Continue tapping while focusing on a specific stressor or feeling of overwhelm.

4. **Move to the Body:** After tapping the karate chop point for approximately 30 seconds, proceed to tap gently on the following body points, spending about five seconds on each:

   - The crown of your head

   - The inner eyebrows

   - The sides of your eyes

   - Under your eyes

   - Under your nose

   - Your chin

   - The beginning of your collarbone

   - Under your arms (about four inches below the armpit)

5. **Maintain Breathing:** As you tap each point, maintain deep, rhythmic breathing. Inhale deeply through your nose before moving to the next tapping point, and exhale through your mouth.

6. **Conclude with Positive Affirmation:** After completing the tapping sequence, place both hands over your heart. Breathe deeply and affirm to yourself, "I am calm, I am relaxed, I am in control," or any other positive affirmation that resonates with you.

7. **Reflect:** Open your eyes and take a moment to notice any changes in your mental or physical state. Acknowledge any reduction in stress or anxiety, however slight it may be.

Common pitfalls:

- **Skipping Breathing Focus:** Neglecting the breathing aspect can reduce the effectiveness of the tapping technique. Ensure to maintain deep, focused breathing throughout the exercise.

- **Rushing Through Points:** Moving too quickly from one tapping point to another without giving yourself time to focus on your feelings and breathe properly can diminish the benefits.

- **Lack of Specificity:** Not focusing on a specific stressor or feeling while tapping may result in less effective stress reduction. Aim to concentrate on a particular source of stress or anxiety.

Progress tracking:

Daily Log: Keep a brief daily log of your stress levels before and after the exercise. Rate your stress on a scale of 1-10 to monitor changes over time.

Reflective Journaling: After each session, jot down any thoughts, feelings, or physical sensations you experienced. Note any shifts in your stress or anxiety levels and any insights gained during the process.

20.2 Overcoming Social Anxiety in Everyday Interactions

Objective: To develop strategies for managing and reducing social anxiety in everyday interactions through guided visualization and grounding techniques, enhancing your ability to engage confidently and calmly in social situations.

Step-by-step instructions:

1. **Find a Quiet Space:** Choose a quiet and comfortable place where you can sit or lie down without interruptions. This space should feel safe and allow you to focus inward without external distractions.

2. **Close Your Eyes and Breathe Deeply:** Close your eyes to shut out the external world. Take deep, slow breaths to center yourself. Inhale through your nose for a count of four, hold for a count of four, and exhale through your mouth for a count of six. Repeat this breathing pattern five times to achieve a state of relaxation.

3. **Visualize a Social Situation:** Imagine a social situation that typically triggers your anxiety. This could be a party, a meeting, or any interaction that usually causes discomfort. Picture this scene as vividly as possible, including the setting, the people present, and the sounds around you.

4. **Identify Your Anxiety:** As you visualize this situation, identify where in your body you feel the anxiety most strongly. Common areas include the chest, stomach, or throat. Acknowledge this sensation without judgment.

5. **Apply Grounding Techniques:** Shift your focus to your feet. Imagine roots growing from the soles of your feet deep into the earth, anchoring you firmly and safely. Feel the strength and stability of the earth supporting you.

6. **Transform the Situation:** In your visualization, begin to alter the situation in a way that makes you feel more comfortable and confident. This could involve imagining yourself speaking fluently, laughing, or being surrounded by supportive people. Notice how your body's sensation of anxiety begins to diminish as the scene changes.

7. **Introduce a Positive Affirmation:** Repeat a positive affirmation to yourself, such as "I am calm and confident in social situations," or "I communicate easily and freely with others." Feel the truth of these words as you continue to breathe deeply.

8. **Gradually Return to the Present:** Slowly bring your awareness back to your current environment. Wiggle your fingers and toes, and when you're ready, open your eyes. Take a moment to notice any changes in how you feel about the social situation you visualized.

Common pitfalls:

- **Skipping the Breathing Exercise:** Neglecting the initial deep breathing exercise can result in less effective visualization and grounding, as deep breathing helps to induce a relaxed state conducive to anxiety management.

- **Rushing Through the Visualization:** Take your time with each step of the visualization to fully immerse yourself in the experience and allow the positive transformation to occur.

- **Ignoring Physical Sensations:** Failing to acknowledge and address the physical sensations associated with anxiety can prevent the full benefit of the exercise, as recognizing these sensations is key to applying effective grounding techniques.

Progress tracking:

Journaling: Keep a journal of your experiences with this exercise, noting the social situations you visualize, your initial and transformed feelings about them, and any changes in your physical sensations of anxiety.

Social Interaction Reflections: After engaging in real-life social situations, reflect on your feelings and behaviors. Compare these to your visualizations to assess progress and areas for further practice.

20.3 Improving Focus and Productivity During the Day

Exercise: Bilateral Stimulation for Enhanced Focus and Productivity

Objective: To enhance focus and productivity through bilateral stimulation, a technique that can help reset and calm the mind, making it easier to concentrate on tasks and improve overall productivity during the day.

Step-by-step instructions:

1. **Find a Quiet Space:** Choose a comfortable and quiet area where you can sit or stand without interruptions for a few minutes.

2. **Start with Deep Breathing:** Before beginning the bilateral stimulation, take a moment to breathe deeply. Inhale slowly through your nose for a count of four, hold your breath for a count of four, and then exhale through your mouth for a count of six. Repeat this breathing exercise three times to help center yourself and prepare for the stimulation exercise.

3. **Engage in Bilateral Tapping:** Use your fingertips to tap gently but firmly on your thighs or knees, alternating between the left and right side. Start with your right hand tapping your right thigh, then your left hand tapping your left thigh, and continue this alternating pattern. Each tap should last for about one second. Continue this tapping sequence for one minute, maintaining a steady rhythm.

4. **Focus on a Single Task:** While tapping, think about a specific task you need to focus on or a project that requires your productivity. Visualize yourself completing this task efficiently and effectively.

5. **Incorporate Positive Affirmations:** After completing the tapping sequence, pause for a moment to affirm your ability to focus and be productive. You can use affirmations such as "I am fully capable of concentrating on my tasks" or "My mind is clear and focused."

6. **Return to Your Task:** After the exercise, immediately return to the task or project you visualized. Notice if you feel more focused and ready to work.

Common pitfalls:

- **Skipping the Breathing Exercise:** Failing to perform the deep breathing exercise before starting the tapping can result in less effectiveness of the bilateral stimulation. The breathing helps to relax the mind and body, making the stimulation more effective.

- **Losing Rhythm in Tapping:** It's important to maintain a consistent rhythm while tapping. Erratic tapping can distract from the focus and reduce the effectiveness of the exercise.

- **Not Focusing on a Specific Task:** The lack of a specific task or project in mind during the tapping sequence may lead to diminished benefits. Having a clear focus enhances the exercise's ability to improve concentration on that particular task.

Progress tracking:

Daily Log: Keep a brief log of your focus and productivity levels before and after performing the exercise each day. Rate your levels on a scale from 1 to 10 to monitor improvements over time.

Task Completion Record: Note down the tasks you focus on during each bilateral stimulation session and record how efficiently you were able to complete them after the exercise compared to previous attempts without the exercise.

20.4 Enhancing Sleep and Evening Relaxation

Objective: To enhance evening relaxation and improve sleep quality through a combination of visualization and tapping techniques, creating a calming bedtime routine that promotes restful sleep.

Step-by-step instructions:

1. **Prepare Your Sleep Environment:** Ensure your bedroom is conducive to sleep - cool, dark, and quiet. Turn off electronic devices at least 30 minutes before your intended sleep time to reduce blue light exposure.

2. **Find a Comfortable Position:** Lie down in your bed in a comfortable position. Allow your body to relax, adjusting your pillows and blankets as needed to feel fully supported.

3. **Begin Deep Breathing:** Close your eyes and focus on your breath. Inhale deeply through your nose for a count of four, hold your breath for a count of seven, then exhale slowly through your mouth for a count of eight. Repeat this breathing pattern four times to initiate relaxation.

4. **Engage in Tapping:** Gently tap your fingertips on your chest, starting from the sternum and moving outward in a circular motion. Continue this gentle tapping for one minute, focusing on the sensation and the rhythm.

5. **Visualize a Peaceful Scene:** While continuing to tap gently, visualize a scene that represents peace and tranquility to you. This could be a quiet beach at sunset, a serene mountain landscape, or any setting that evokes a sense of calm. Immerse yourself in this visualization, noting any sounds, smells, or sensations associated with this place.

6. **Incorporate Positive Sleep Affirmations:** Silently repeat affirmations that reinforce your ability to sleep well. Use phrases like "I am calm and relaxed," "My body knows how to fall asleep naturally," or "Each breath takes me deeper into a state of sleep."

7. **Gradually Wind Down the Tapping:** Slowly reduce the frequency of your tapping until you stop. Continue to breathe deeply and maintain the visualization of your peaceful scene.

8. **Release the Visualization:** Gently let go of your visualized scene, maintaining the sense of calm and relaxation it brought you. Allow yourself to drift into sleep, carried by the calmness and the comfort of your bed.

Common pitfalls:

- **Becoming Frustrated if Sleep Doesn't Come Immediately:** It's normal for sleep to take time, especially when trying a new routine. Be patient and gentle with yourself, allowing the process to unfold naturally.

- **Overthinking the Steps:** The goal is relaxation, not perfection. If you find yourself focusing too much on getting the steps right, take a few deep breaths and gently bring your focus back to the sensations of relaxation.

Progress tracking:

Sleep Journal: Keep a sleep journal beside your bed to note any changes in your sleep patterns, how quickly you fall asleep, and the quality of your sleep after incorporating this exercise into your routine.

Reflect on Relaxation Levels: Periodically, reflect on your levels of relaxation and ease of falling asleep since beginning this exercise. Note any improvements or areas where you might need to adjust your approach.

Chapter 21: Synergizing EMDR with Complementary Therapies

21.1: Exploring Somatic Therapies and EMDR

Integrating Eye Movement Desensitization and Reprocessing (EMDR) with somatic therapies offers a holistic approach to healing that acknowledges the interconnectedness of mind and body. Somatic therapies focus on the body's sensations and movements to help release stored trauma and emotional distress. When combined with EMDR, these therapies can enhance the therapeutic process, offering a comprehensive path to recovery and emotional well-being.

Somatic Experiencing (SE), for instance, is a body-focused approach that helps individuals renegotiate and heal trauma rather than relive it. By paying close attention to bodily sensations and employing gentle exercises to release tension, SE facilitates the completion of self-protective motor responses that were thwarted at the time of trauma. Incorporating EMDR's structured protocol with SE's focus on bodily sensations allows for a deeper processing of traumatic memories, making it possible to address both the psychological and somatic effects of trauma.

Body-Mind Centering (BMC) is another somatic practice that can be synergized with EMDR. BMC explores how psychological, emotional, and cognitive states are expressed through the body. The practice involves guided movement, touch, and voice exercises to foster awareness and transformation at the cellular level. When paired with EMDR, BMC can help individuals develop a more integrated sense of self, enhancing the effectiveness of trauma processing by engaging the body's innate wisdom and capacity for healing.

Breathwork is a powerful somatic technique that can be integrated into EMDR therapy. Controlled breathing exercises can regulate the nervous system and reduce symptoms of anxiety and stress. Breathwork can prepare individuals for EMDR sessions by helping them achieve a relaxed state, making it easier to access and process traumatic memories. Additionally, incorporating breathwork after EMDR sessions can assist in grounding and stabilizing emotions, facilitating a smoother integration of the session's work.

Yoga, with its emphasis on mindful movement and breath, offers another complementary practice to EMDR. Yoga poses and sequences can help release physical tension and improve body awareness. The practice of yoga can support the EMDR process by helping individuals develop a stronger connection with their bodies, which is often disrupted by trauma. The mindfulness aspect of yoga also aligns with EMDR's aim to foster a present-centered state of awareness, which is crucial for effective trauma processing.

To effectively integrate EMDR with somatic therapies, therapists should be trained in both modalities and understand how to blend them seamlessly to support the client's healing journey. This integration offers a more nuanced approach to therapy, recognizing that trauma and emotional distress manifest in both the mind and the body. By addressing these aspects simultaneously, individuals can achieve a more profound and lasting recovery, moving beyond trauma to a place of greater emotional freedom and resilience.

21.2: Combining EMDR and CBT Techniques

Combining Eye Movement Desensitization and Reprocessing (EMDR) with Cognitive-Behavioral Techniques (CBT) creates a powerful synergy for addressing dysfunctional beliefs and fostering lasting change. This approach integrates the strengths of both therapies to target the underlying cognitive, emotional, and physiological aspects of psychological distress. EMDR focuses on desensitizing distressing memories and reprocessing them to reduce their lingering effects, while CBT aims to change negative thought patterns and behaviors that arise from these memories. Together, they offer a comprehensive framework for healing.

EMDR's Role in Cognitive and Emotional Reprocessing:

EMDR therapy facilitates the accessing and reprocessing of traumatic memories, leading to a decrease in emotional distress and the reformulation of negative beliefs. Through its structured phases, EMDR helps individuals confront and reprocess traumatic memories, reducing their emotional charge and enabling the development of more adaptive coping mechanisms. This process is crucial for altering the negative beliefs that are often at the core of psychological issues.

CBT's Contribution to Thought and Behavior Modification:

CBT techniques are instrumental in identifying, challenging, and modifying negative thought patterns and behaviors. By incorporating CBT strategies, individuals learn to recognize their automatic negative thoughts and assess their validity. This cognitive restructuring is essential for replacing dysfunctional beliefs with more realistic and positive ones, leading to healthier behaviors and emotional responses.

Synergizing EMDR and CBT:

To effectively combine EMDR and CBT, therapists may follow a phased approach:

1. **Assessment and History Taking**:
   Identify the individual's specific negative beliefs and the traumatic memories associated with them.

2. **Preparation**:
   Use CBT techniques to build coping skills for emotional regulation and stress management, preparing the individual for the EMDR reprocessing phases.

3. **Desensitization and Reprocessing**:
   Apply EMDR to target and reprocess traumatic memories, reducing their emotional impact.

4. **Cognitive Restructuring**:
   Following EMDR, employ CBT strategies to challenge and modify the negative beliefs that were reinforced by the traumatic experiences.

5. **Behavioral Experiments**:
   Encourage the individual to test out new beliefs in real-life situations, reinforcing the cognitive shifts made during therapy.

6. **Consolidation and Future Planning**:
   Use both EMDR and CBT techniques to reinforce positive beliefs and coping strategies, ensuring lasting change.

Practical Application:

For instance, an individual struggling with the belief "I am powerless" stemming from a traumatic event may first undergo EMDR to reduce the distress linked to that event. Following this, CBT techniques can be used to identify instances where the individual has demonstrated power and control, challenging and reshaping the belief into "I have the power to affect change in my life."

Enhancing Therapy with Bilateral Stimulation:

Incorporating bilateral stimulation, a core component of EMDR, during the cognitive restructuring phase of CBT can enhance the integration of new, positive beliefs. This stimulation can facilitate deeper processing of these beliefs, making them more salient and accessible.

Conclusion: By integrating EMDR and CBT, therapists can offer a more dynamic and multifaceted approach to healing. This combination not only addresses the root cause of psychological distress but also equips individuals with the cognitive and behavioral tools necessary for ongoing growth and resilience. As such, this synergistic approach can be particularly effective for those whose psychological distress is maintained by both unresolved trauma and dysfunctional cognitive patterns.

Conclusion

22. Celebrating Your Progress

As you reflect on your journey with EMDR, consider the profound changes you've initiated in your life. The transformation from feeling overwhelmed by stress and anxiety to a state of emotional freedom and resilience is a testament to your dedication and the power of these therapeutic techniques. The process of Eye Movement Desensitization and Reprocessing has offered you tools not just for coping, but for thriving in the face of life's challenges. The adaptive information processing model, central to EMDR, has illuminated the path for reprocessing memories that once seemed insurmountable, allowing you to reframe your narrative towards one of strength and positivity.

The practice of creating a safe space, both mentally and physically, has become a cornerstone of your daily routine, providing a sanctuary from the stresses of the world. This concept, fundamental to the EMDR process, serves as a reminder of the importance of self-care and the need to prioritize your emotional well-being. Grounding techniques, such as deep breathing and mindfulness, have become tools in your arsenal to combat the onset of anxiety, enabling you to remain present and focused. The bilateral stimulation exercises, whether through eye movements or tapping, have taught you to balance your emotional and cognitive states, fostering a sense of inner harmony.

Your journey through the eight phases of EMDR therapy has been transformative, each step building upon the last to deepen your understanding of yourself and your reactions to past traumas. The initial phases of history taking and treatment planning laid the groundwork for your healing, emphasizing the importance of a collaborative approach to therapy. As you progressed to the phases of desensitization and reprocessing, you learned to confront and reframe your traumatic memories, reducing their power over your present emotions and behaviors.

The installation of positive beliefs has been a pivotal phase, replacing negative self-perceptions with affirmations of your worth and capabilities. This shift in mindset has not only improved your self-esteem but has also opened up new avenues for personal growth and fulfillment. The body scan phase further connected you to the physical manifestations of your emotional pain, teaching you to release tension and embrace a state of relaxation.

As you navigated the closure and reevaluation phases, you gained insights into the importance of balance and ongoing self-assessment. These stages reinforced the concept that healing is a continuous journey, one that requires patience, persistence, and self-compassion. The skills and strategies you've acquired through EMDR have not only equipped you to face past traumas but have also prepared you for the challenges and opportunities that lie ahead.

Your exploration of EMDR has extended beyond the therapy sessions, incorporating self-help techniques into your daily life. Bilateral tapping, guided visualizations, and the practice of safe eye movements have become part of your toolkit for managing everyday stress and anxiety. These practices have empowered you to take control of your emotional well-being, fostering a sense of autonomy and confidence in your ability to navigate life's ups and downs.

The impact of EMDR on your relationships cannot be overstated. The improvement in communication, empathy, and emotional connection has enriched your interactions with others, building stronger, more meaningful bonds. The exercises designed to strengthen connections and foster empathy have highlighted the importance of understanding and compassion in all your relationships, whether personal or professional.

As you stand at this juncture, reflecting on the progress you've made, it's clear that the journey with EMDR is far from over. The principles and techniques you've learned are not just for overcoming past traumas but are tools for life, guiding you towards a future filled with hope, resilience, and emotional freedom. The next chapter of your journey beckons, promising new opportunities for growth, healing, and transformation.

Embracing these principles and techniques as part of your ongoing personal development strategy, you are equipped to face not only the remnants of past traumas but also the stresses and strains of everyday life. The adaptability of the EMDR framework allows for its application in a myriad of scenarios, beyond those strictly defined by trauma, to include managing the anxieties of daily life, enhancing personal and professional relationships, and fostering an environment conducive to growth and self-improvement.

The concept of a "safe space" has evolved for you, from a psychological necessity during therapy to a metaphor for creating a life where you feel secure, valued, and understood. This evolution reflects a broader transition from healing to thriving, where the skills learned through EMDR therapy become part of a larger toolkit for emotional intelligence and resilience.

Your ability to apply grounding techniques in moments of stress, to use bilateral stimulation to regain emotional equilibrium, and to employ visualization for positive self-reinforcement, demonstrates a profound mastery over your internal landscape. This mastery is not an endpoint but a foundation upon which you can build an ever-more fulfilling life.

The journey through the phases of EMDR therapy has instilled in you a deep understanding of the interconnectedness of thoughts, emotions, and bodily sensations, highlighting the importance of holistic self-care practices. This understanding encourages a balanced approach to wellness, integrating physical, emotional, and mental health into a cohesive whole.

Moreover, the impact of EMDR on your relationships has taught you the value of empathy, active listening, and open communication, enriching your interactions and connections with others. These skills extend beyond personal relationships to enhance professional interactions, contributing to a more harmonious and productive environment.

As you continue to apply these techniques and insights, remember that the journey of personal growth and emotional healing is ongoing. The landscape of your life will change, presenting new challenges and opportunities for growth. The tools and strategies you've acquired through EMDR equip you to navigate these changes with grace and resilience, turning potential obstacles into stepping stones for further development.

Your exploration of EMDR has been transformative, providing not only relief from past burdens but also a framework for continuous personal evolution. This framework is adaptable, capable of being tailored to meet your changing needs and circumstances. As you move forward, the principles of EMDR can serve as a guiding light, illuminating the path to a future where emotional freedom and fulfillment are not just aspirations but lived realities.

The journey with EMDR is a testament to your strength, resilience, and commitment to personal growth. As you embark on the next chapter of your life, carry forward the lessons learned, the skills honed, and the insights gained. These tools are not just for overcoming trauma but for enriching your entire life experience, enabling you to live with greater awareness, purpose, and joy.

Made in the USA
Middletown, DE
04 April 2025

73757371R00090